Lies, Deception and Truth

Also by Ann E. Weiss

GOD AND GOVERNMENT
The Separation of Church and State

TUNE IN, TUNE OUT
Broadcasting Regulation in the United States

THE NUCLEAR ARMS RACE
Can We Survive It?

GOOD NEIGHBORS?
The United States and Latin America

MONEY GAMES
The Business of Sports

Lies, Deception and Truth

Ann E. Weiss

Houghton Mifflin Company
Boston

Library of Congress Cataloging-in-Publication Data

Weiss, Ann E., 1943–
  Lies, deception, and truth / Ann E. Weiss.
    p.   cm.
  Bibliography: p.
  Includes index.
  Summary: An investigation of the nature of truth, ethics, and
deception.
    HC ISBN 0-395-40486-X   PA ISBN 0-395-65750-4
    1. Truthfulness and falsehood—Juvenile literature. 2. Deception—
Juvenile literature. [1. Honesty.]
BJ1421.W45   1988   88-17534
177'.3—dc 19   CIP
                        AC

Printed in the United States of America

AGM 10 9 8 7 6 5 4 3 2 1

To my parents

Contents

Author's Note

Want to be the center of attention? The focus of animated conversation? Simply announce to any gathering of people that you are writing a book on the subject of lies and deception.

Everyone will be impressed. And everyone will have a different idea about the form the book should take. Your friend the law student will talk about the intriguing cases her legal ethics professor analyzed last semester. Her husband the scientist will interrupt with tales of questionable research procedures. The banker in the group will bring up shady financial dealings, and someone else will mention this month's state house scandal. An elementary school teacher will advise you to check out misleading television advertising aimed at young viewers. Your mother will recall a certain unfortunate incident from your own past. . . .

That scenario is not much of an exaggeration. Soon after undertaking this project, I mentioned it to a group of librarians, educators and other writers. Their enthusiasm was gratifying — and almost overwhelming. Within minutes, thirty-odd people were urging roughly the same number of different approaches: concentrate on politics; keep the book light; limit yourself to school and family situations; make it broad in scope. Any one of those approaches might have worked perfectly well; to follow them all was clearly impossible. Which lies — which types of lies — were most significant? I wondered. People fib about so many things under so many circumstances. Which most needed to be covered? Which could be ignored?

Such were the questions with which I struggled while working on the first draft of this book. It was an unsatisfactory draft, because these questions were not the ones that most needed asking. Only months later — and only after a ream and a half of typing paper had been consigned to the wastebasket — did more relevant questions begin emerging. Among them: *Why* do people sometimes resort to deception? How do they explain or justify doing so? How do others react to those justifications? With questions like these shaping my writing, the second draft was a marked improvement over the first.

Even so, much paper remained to be sacrificed to this book. For it was only in recognizing the need to write a third, and final, draft that I finally understood that I was dealing not just with lies and deception but with honesty and ethics as well. That's because people do not tell lies only in order to get others to believe that which is not the truth. They may also lie in order to serve the truth, or what they believe the truth to be. The central dilemma of human deception, it seemed, is this: we believe that it is wrong or sinful to lie. Equally strongly, we believe that there are times when lying is the only right — the only *truthful* — thing to do. The question is not just, When is it right to deviate from the truth? but also, What is the truth to begin with?

A subject like this is not easily written about. In tackling it, I was helped enormously by Sissela Bok's book *Lying: Moral Choice in Public and Private Life,* which I mention several times in the text. Other sources (in addition to the informal ones referred to above) included a number of periodicals: *The New York Times, The Christian Science Monitor, The New Scientist, Time* magazine and *The Nation* among them. I also must express my gratitude to my family and friends, who put up with a good deal of bad temper during the more difficult stages of the preparation of this book, and to my editor, Matilda Welter, who, after all, had to plow through all those drafts!

A. E. W.

Lies, Deception and Truth

1
Sheriff Hackett and Mr. J. B. Dunn

The letters, typed on the stationery of the U.S.A. Cable Television Network, were signed by a J. B. Dunn. They were mailed out from Jay, New York, in mid-November, and arrived at two hundred addresses in central Maine's Kennebec County just before Thanksgiving Day. Each contained an exciting offer: free lunch and dinner and a chance to appear in a network documentary about life in the Maine countryside.

"Our computer has selected you as one of the many citizens that we will be interested in interviewing while we are in Maine," the letters said. "We would like to hear your thoughts, feelings, opinions and experiences of growing up and living in one of this country's most beautiful and rural areas." Payment for each interview would be "at the standard rate." Those who wished to participate were instructed to show up at the Holiday Inn in Augusta — capital of Maine and the county seat — the following Saturday morning.

Six people did show up, each delighted by the break in routine and intrigued by the prospect of being on television. Grasping their precious letters, they hurried into the motel, eager to meet J. B. Dunn and to experience television's behind-the-scenes glamour for themselves. What a lucky opportunity had come their way! What a break!

What a shock.

Entering the motel room as instructed, each of the six stopped short. There to greet them was not Mr. Dunn but Frank Hackett, Jr., the recently elected sheriff of Kennebec County. He was surrounded not by reporters, camera crews and sound and lighting technicians but by eleven brawny deputy sheriffs. And instead of two expense-account meals and a generous paycheck, each of those who had walked so trustingly into the Holiday Inn was handed an arrest warrant. It was in a court of law that each was slated to appear, not on a television screen. The whole setup — letters, TV offer, promised meals, everything — had been a trick, a hoax. A lie.

It was a lie that Sheriff Hackett was happy to dissect later for news reporters. Each of the two hundred men and women who received a letter had previously failed to appear in court to answer the charges against him or her. The charges ranged from ignoring speeding tickets to driving while intoxicated to burglary. Attempts by

Kennebec County deputies to pick up these men and women at home had met with no success, as the accused had frequently changed their addresses or taken refuge with friends and relatives. "We felt if we devised something like this we'd be able to get people to come to us, rather than us coming to them," Hackett said, adding that some of the warrants had been outstanding for over ten years. By his account, the sheriff had inherited a total of four hundred unanswered warrants upon taking office the year before. "We're going to clean this list up," he vowed.

Hackett was also glad to reveal the mechanics of the hoax. The "U.S.A. Cable Television Network" was a fabrication, of course. "U.S.A." stood for "You Should have Appeared" and "J. B. Dunn" for "Justice Be Done." After the letters had been written and signed, they were bundled up and sent via United Parcel Service to Hackett's brother, a New York resident. The brother took them to a local post office and mailed them back to Maine. This stratagem was a vital piece of the deception, since it ensured a postmark from a part of the country where a national cable network might be supposed to have its headquarters.

The sheriff's "sting" operation aroused a great deal of comment, much of it unfavorable. "Too expensive" was the commonest complaint. How much had it cost to print, ship and mail the letters? How much for the motel room? How much for manpower? Sheriff Hackett and eleven of his deputies had each devoted over five hours to the operation.

Another objection concerned the motives behind the deception. A publicity-hungry Hackett had chosen this way of tracking down the elusive wrongdoers, his critics charged, as a means of winning attention in the news media and more votes in the next election. And how many warrants had actually been cleared up by his unorthodox methods? Fewer than half a dozen. What Hackett and his men should have done, many argued, was to have followed routine police procedure, plodding away from address to address, rounding up the wanted people. But no, instead of buckling down to hard work, Hackett had opted for a flashy, headline-making gimmick.

A third, and more poignant, criticism came from one of those who had been taken in by the hoax, a man named William Fullerton. Like Hackett, Fullerton was quick to share his story with reporters. He described to them how he had arrived at the Holiday Inn at the appointed hour to be welcomed by a man posing as a network employee. "He asked me what I did for work," Fullerton recalled, "and told me that I looked like the type of person who would be good in this movie — like an outdoor person. He . . . said in a few minutes I would be interviewed by the other fellows. A few minutes went by and they called me in.'' Fullerton was served with a warrant.

"I asked him what is it I was supposed to have done. He told me some traffic violations and fines I hadn't paid.''

Fullerton knew right away that a mistake had been made. It was his *son* the sheriff was looking for, he explained to the deputy. The younger Fullerton was the one with the violations. An on-the-spot comparison of birth dates showed that this was the case.

For Fullerton, the error meant more than a wasted morning. He had undergone a humiliating experience that probed painfully at old wounds. Not only had he nearly been arrested for offenses he never committed, but the incident also served as a reminder of the fact that his son had left home and lost touch with his family.

Almost as bad as that reminder was the letdown Fullerton felt after the deputies sent him home. He had been ill and depressed for some time, Fullerton told reporters, and the idea that his "thoughts, feelings, opinions and experiences" were unique and meaningful and would prove of interest to others had been a terrific morale-booster. It had made him feel — for a little while — better about himself and his life. Now that good feeling was destroyed. "The part about 'Justice Be Done' — was justice done in my case?'' he demanded.

Hackett had to admit it had not been. He apologized to Fullerton, but continued to defend the sting operation itself. "We weren't doing it to hurt anyone," he argued. "We were doing it to make Kennebec County a safer place to live." As he reminded the press, a number of the warrants concerned allegations of serious crimes, like theft, or of life-threatening ones, such as drunk driving. In his view, men and women accused of activities like these must be forced into court, no matter how unusual the tactics used to get them there.

What was more, he asserted, his tactics were not actually all that unusual. He was not the first to employ them, and they were well within the law. Hackett had checked that out with Maine's attorney general, the state's chief law officer, before going ahead with his plan. Similar stings have been found to be legal in other states, too.

Even the federal government has used the sting tactics to locate missing offenders. At about the time of the Augusta operation, U.S. marshals in Washington, D.C., invited three thousand fugitives to a party, promising each of them two free passes to a pro football game between the Washington Redskins and the Cincinnati Bengals. The hundred men who fell for the scam were welcomed by one person in a yellow chicken suit and another dressed as an Indian chief, headdress and all. Under the disguises, both were marshals. Tuxedo-clad "waiters" — also marshals — circulated through the crowd, handing out name tags. Then the hundred "guests" were herded aboard buses, ostensibly to head for the game. Their journey ended a few blocks away at the city jail.

Maine's Sheriff Hackett also had a response for those who scoffed that a scheme so elaborate had netted a catch of only five. In the days following the operation, he announced, several other Kennebec County residents who had received J. B. Dunn letters turned themselves in to his department. Even though they had not been fooled by the phony offer, these people were plainly convinced that the aggressive young sheriff was bound to track them down eventually anyway. In all, nearly two dozen old warrants were removed from the books as a direct result of the sting. Finally, the cost of the operation turned out to have been minimal — $105 for stationery and $58 for shipping and mailing the letters. Hackett and his deputies had donated their time that Saturday morning, and the manager of the Holiday Inn did not charge for the use of the room.

That settled it. The controversy died down. The next year, Sheriff Hackett was re-elected by a large majority, and before long he was carrying out other deceptions aimed at clearing up more of the county's outstanding warrants. And by that time no one was raising any questions about his methods.

One question never had been raised, of course, not even during the first flurry of controversy over Sheriff

Hackett's tactics. Nor does that question seem to have come up in other places where law enforcement officers have employed similar means to catch wrongdoers. People have expressed concern about the expense of such operations and about their legality. They have brought up the possibility that the motivation behind them is mere laziness or publicity seeking. But few have thought to ponder the stings' ethical implications. Few have wondered whether or not it is moral for government officials to seek to protect the public and enforce the law by engaging in deception. Rarely has anyone asked: Is it right to lie?

2
Deception and Human Nature

Is it right to lie? Any four-year-old knows the answer to that one: no. Good boys and girls don't lie — that is among the first things children learn from their parents. They learn the same from their teachers and from the ministers, priests, rabbis and others charged with helping to direct their religious and moral training. Never tell a lie, everyone says.

As teenagers and adults, people continue to be made aware of their obligation to be truthful. High school or college administrators may compel students to sign honor codes designed to discourage them from cheating in class or engaging in other dishonest practices. Clubs and fraternal organizations emphasize the importance of truthfulness. Anyone testifying in a court of law must take a solemn oath to tell the truth. Associations of doctors, lawyers, businesspeople and others commonly adopt ethical standards that members are expected to meet. Men and women elected to public office swear to uphold the law of the land — another way of promising to be honest.

On a personal level, too, people know that honesty is required of them. "Say what you really think," a friend commands. "Don't lie to me about this," a sister warns. People set up standards of truthfulness for themselves, as well. "To be completely frank with you," they say, or "I'm not going to pretend about this." The truth, the whole truth and nothing but the truth — that and nothing less is the ideal.

Is it an ideal anyone could hope to live up to? Can you imagine never telling a lie? Never uttering an insincere compliment or a polite social fib? Never exaggerating to put a better face on things? Never pretending to have fulfilled an obligation, trying to hide a mistake or seeking to avoid punishment?

Or try to imagine a world in which no one else ever lies. No friend or family member, no teacher, no boss, no rival, no salesperson or advertiser or politician — no one. Impossible? Of course. Just think of the news stories Americans were reading and hearing about as the 1980s drew to a close. Some of the nation's largest universities forced to admit that teachers and coaches had lied about the poor grades of star athletes. Executives at major corporations paying fines imposed upon them as a result of their having advertised their products with false claims. One former United States senator and likely presidential contender gone from the political campaign after newspaper publicity about his false denials of affairs with women other than his wife; and a second contender in the same race eliminated when it became known that he had cribbed parts of other politicians' speeches and lied about his law school record. Well-known television preachers found to have profited personally from the millions of dollars sent in as contributions from the faithful. The list goes on and on, leading one national news magazine, *Time*, to demand in the headline to a 1987 cover story: "Whatever Happened to Ethics?"

Whatever indeed. All of us know that we, and others, are supposed to be honest. But we also know that whatever parents, teachers, public officials, religious leaders and moralists may say, falsehood and deception are part of human life.

It has been that way from the start. According to Judeo-Christian tradition, human civilization began with a lie, the serpent's lie to Eve in the Garden of Eden. God had warned Adam and Eve that if they ate from the tree of knowledge, they would perish. But the treacherous serpent sought to deceive Eve. "Ye shall not surely die," he told her, and Eve believed him and ate.

The serpent was not the only liar in the garden. After Adam and Eve recognized their nakedness and covered themselves with fig leaves, God challenged them. "Who told thee that thou wast naked? Hast thou eaten of the tree?'' Whereupon Adam, instead of answering with a forthright yes, responded indirectly. "The woman thou gavest to be with me," he said, "she gave me of the tree." His words were literally true. Eve had offered to share the forbidden fruit with Adam. She didn't force it on him, though. The decision to eat was Adam's own, but fearing God's anger, he tried to lay the entire responsibility on Eve. An oblique lie is just as dishonest as an outright misstatement of fact.

Naturally, God was not fooled and he banished Adam from paradise along with Eve. And so it was upon two lies — one direct and the other by implication — that the human condition, and the pain and sorrow to which God condemned mankind, were founded. Or so the Bible tells us.

The gates of the Garden of Eden sealed behind them, human beings continued their lying ways. Time passed, and Adam and Eve had two sons, Cain and Abel. The boys grew into men, and Cain became jealous of Abel and slew him. When God inquired as to Abel's whereabouts, Cain answered as his father had done before him, with an evasion. "Am I my brother's keeper?" Again, God was not deceived. He punished Cain by placing the mark of the murderer upon him and driving him away to wander the face of the earth.

Further on in the book of Genesis, we read of another deception, this one so complex that it could not rest upon the spoken word alone. When Isaac, the son of Abraham, lay nearly blind and dying, he called his firstborn, Esau, to him. "Make me savoury meat," Isaac commanded, "that I may eat; that my soul may bless thee before I die." Obediently, Esau went out with his bow and arrows to hunt for venison.

But Isaac's wife, Rebekah, overheard this and called her favorite son, Jacob, to her. I will fix meat the way your father likes it best, she told him, and you take it to him and pretend to be Esau. Then you will be the one to earn his last blessing and the wealth and worldly power that will flow from that blessing. Jacob was willing, but he foresaw a practical problem. He was smooth-skinned, he reminded Rebekah, while Esau was hairy. "My father . . . will feel me," Jacob warned, "and I shall seem to him as a deceiver; and I shall bring a curse upon me and not a blessing." The resourceful Rebekah, however, had a plan. She dressed Jacob in Esau's clothing, then covered his hands and "the smooth of his neck" with rough goatskins. Attired in this fashion, Jacob brought the meat to Isaac and told him, "I am Esau, thy firstborn."

Isaac accepted the lie. His faith in Jacob's words was reinforced when he felt the hairy goatskins and smelled the distinctive odor of Esau's clothes. The deception worked — until Esau returned home with his own offering of meat.

These Old Testament stories illustrate, among other things, how inventive humans can be when it comes to deception. People can lie with words; directly, as the serpent lied to Eve, or indirectly, like Adam and Cain. They can create visual deceptions, the way Jacob did when he put on Esau's coat, and deceive through touch and smell. Even taste can be involved. The food that Rebekah prepared for Jacob to give to Isaac was actually goat meat, but Isaac, already convinced by his other senses, believed it to be venison. Jacob got his blessing.

Modern liars are no less ingenious than ancient ones, as we will see throughout this book. They lie verbally with words and visually with staged scenes and altered photographs — even with doctored films and video-tapes. They try to deceive using numbers and statistics and by means of false smiles and other misleading "body language." They convey misinformation in jokes and anecdotes, and conceal vital truths through silence and censorship. They produce fakes, forgeries and counter-feits. They disguise vice as virtue and parade advertis-ing and propaganda, including political propaganda, as factual information. They employ spies and secret dou-ble agents. The ways of human deception are myriad indeed.

To some people, those ways seem to be not merely part of human nature but a part of all nature. Lying did not begin in the Garden of Eden with Adam and Eve, they believe, nor with any other human beings. It goes further back than that, to a time before human life existed. The natural world is itself deceptive, these people say, and when we humans lie we are only showing that we are a part of that world and inexorably bound to it.

Are they right? Is dishonesty among human beings unavoidable and inescapable, an inevitable consequence of being alive on this planet? It is certainly true that deceptions are to be found throughout the natural world. Take a plant like the Venus's-flytrap, for example. Although Venus's-flytraps contain no substances upon which flies or other insects would care to feed, they look and smell very much like plants that do. Examined under ultraviolet light, some trapping plants even reveal the characteristic patterns, invisible to humans in ordinary light, that are so attractive to foraging insects. When such an insect is fooled and lights on the plant — snap! *It* becomes the meal.

Just as intricate is the illusion created by a fungus known as *Monilinia vaciniicorymbosi*. *Monilinia* invades the blueberry plant, establishing itself on the leaves. It cannot reproduce, however, unless its spores reach the plant's flowers. Although the wind may move the spores eventually, a more efficient means of transportation would be a bee. But since bees are not normally attracted to leaves, *Monilinia* has evolved a trick. As it grows, it gives the plant's leaves much the same appearance, smell and taste as its flowers. Deceived by the mimicry, a bee lands on a leaf, picks up some of the spores on its fuzzy body, then buzzes away to the plant's true blooms. An animal, too, can deceive by its appearance. Natural camouflage allows snakes, lizards, moths and many other creatures to blend in with their surroundings, effectively disguising them from predators or prey, or both.

But can the "deceptions" of animal camouflage and the misleading appearance of some plants be compared in any way to human deceit? Many would argue that they cannot. The deceptions we human beings practice upon one another are deliberate and consciously devised, they point out, and that sets them completely apart from the unconscious deceptions of plants and animals.

Yet some animal deceptions do appear to have at least an element of more or less conscious intent, scientists are learning. In a report published in a 1986 issue of the British magazine *Nature,* Charles A. Munn of the New York Zoological Society described the highly deceptive animal behavior he observed in the jungles of South America.

Dr. Munn's observations were of birds of two slightly different species, the white-winged tanager-shrike and the antshrike. Each shrike has its own distinct warning call, which members of the species use to alert each other to danger — from a predatory hawk circling overhead, for instance. But each species is able to imitate the other's warning, and according to Dr. Munn, each uses this ability deceptively in the hunt for food. Over and over, he wrote, an antshrike would appear in hot pursuit of an insect, usually a katydid. Just as the bird was about to gulp the bug, a tanager-shrike would sound the antshrike warning cry. Distracted, the antshrike would lose sight of the katydid. The tanager-shrike would then swoop in and grab it. At other times, Dr. Munn watched as antshrikes were the ones to sound the false alarm and steal the food.

Are the deceptions of the South American shrikes deliberate in the way that human deceptions are? Dr. Munn is not sure. "I have no reason not to think they know what they are doing," he says, phrasing the thought rather awkwardly. "But I can't prove it."

There can be little doubt, however, that an animal as advanced as the chimpanzee does possess such awareness. British scientist Jane Goodall has spent years studying chimps in a remote part of the East African nation of Tanzania. Her close observations of the animals' behavior in the wild are probably more detailed than those of any other scientist, and as early as the 1970s, she was reporting what seemed to be intentional deception among them. In one case, she saw a male chimp who had located a bunch of bananas lead a group of other chimps away from the food, then return to gorge alone. That sounds remarkably like the fourth-grader who distracts her little brother's attention from a plate of cookies while plotting to gobble them up at the first opportunity. Since the seventies, other scientists have spotted similar instances of deceptive chimp behavior. "Deception seems to permeate all aspects of chimpanzee social life," says Frans de Waal of the University of Wisconsin. It is a kind of behavior that many scientists believe to be similar to intentional human deception.

Some scientists go so far as to suggest that not only is a drive to deceive part of all nature but that deceit may also have played a role in human evolution. Two American anthropologists, Jeffrey A. Kurland and Stephen J. Beckerman of Pennsylvania State University, point out that the search for food must have been one factor that bound the earliest human beings into primitive societies and led them to develop languages. The need to share information about scarce resources would have encouraged such cooperation and communication, a number of scientists agree.

But beyond that, Kurland and Beckerman go on, "systems of reciprocity" — mutual dependence — "seem open to subtle cheating." In other words, early humans, like the deceitful chimp observed by Dr. Goodall, probably held out on other members of the group from time to time. Those long-ago men and women who could both find a food supply and keep that supply for themselves — and perhaps for a mate and their offspring — gained an advantage over those who could not. That advantage could help make them the best fed, and therefore the healthiest and strongest, in the community. Their health and strength, in turn, would mean they would be the ones most likely to survive and to pass their talents, and the deceptive tricks they had learned, on to future generations. Eventually, "the overall pressure to receive accurate information and transmit less than . . . accurate information becomes enormous," Kurland and Beckerman write. Lying, they say, could have been a tool of survival.

Many people find this notion — that the drive to lie and deceive may have been locked into human nature by the very process of evolution — deeply disturbing. Yet is this point of view so different from the idea that it was deception in the Garden of Eden that helped set the stage for the fall of man and the launching of civilization? The Bible story, too, suggests that lying is a fundamental human trait. Men and women who regard the biblical account of the creation as fact and those who accept the idea of the evolution of species are far apart in their thinking, but they do seem to agree on this much: that to lie and seek to deceive are part of what it means to be a human being.

Why, then, do people regard lying as wrong? Why do they place so high a value on the truth?

3
Truth, Religion and Philosophy

Truth is essential to life and to society. Without it, there would be nothing — not even lies.

That may sound peculiar, but think about it. No lie will work — be accepted as true — unless the person who is to be deceived anticipates being presented with the truth. Isaac, for instance, expected the truth from his wife and sons. He did not doubt that when someone said to him, "I am Esau, thy firstborn," that person really would turn out to be Esau. If Isaac had suspected that his family might be deceitful, he would have been much harder to fool. He might have peered longer and harder at the false Esau and spotted him as Jacob despite his failing vision. He might have wondered at the extreme roughness and hairiness of the young man's hands and neck. Surely, if he had had any lack of confidence at all in his son's honesty, he would have recognized the taste of the goat meat. But Isaac did not lack confidence. He trusted in the truthfulness of those around him, and that is why Jacob's hoax worked.

Deception works in nature for the same reason. Bees are attracted to certain flower elements — their smell, their color, their distinctive patterns and so on. In rare instances they can be fooled into accepting another part of a plant as its flower, and as we saw in chapter 2, a fungus like *Monilinia vaciniicorymbosi* may take advantage of a bee's "gullibility" to enhance its own chances at reproduction. But suppose *Monilinia* disguised not just a few blueberry leaves but every leaf. At first, bees would be fooled over and over, moving from "flower" to "flower" and finding no pollen. But how long would it be before the insects gave up on the blueberries and flew off to other, more "honest" blossoms? *Monilinia*'s deception works only because most of the time bees do find blueberry pollen where they expect it. The same is true in the case of the South American shrike species that imitate each other's warning calls. Unless a bird accepts the cry as a genuine danger signal, it will not be distracted from its prey. If the calls are not usually honest, the false ones will eventually go unheeded and the birds uttering them will be like the boy who cried "wolf" once too often. "For deception to succeed," concludes Robert W. Mitchell, a psychologist at Clark University in Massachusetts and the author of a book called *Deception: Perspectives on Human and Nonhuman Deceit*, "there has to be some grounding in truth."

So truth is essential. Even when lies are used as tools

of survival — in the search for food or to ensure efficient reproduction, for example — those lies cannot stand except upon a solid foundation of truth and trust. Plant, animal and human survival may owe something to deception, but fundamentally all three depend on honesty. The need to deceive on occasion may be part of human nature, may even be built into that nature, but underlying that need is an overwhelming necessity for truth. How do we reconcile the contradiction?

One way is through religious belief. All the world's major faiths are centered upon an idea of truth. Hinduism, the religion whose roots can be traced furthest back in human history, recognizes many different gods but regards each of them as one aspect of a Supreme Being who embodies all reality and all truth. The ancient Hebrews were the first to adopt monotheism, the worship of a single God. That God, Moses sang to his people over three thousand years ago, "is the Rock, his work is perfect, a God of truth and without iniquity, just and right is he." Twelve hundred years later, Jesus of Nazareth told his disciples, "I am the way, the truth, and the life," and upon that truth, Christianity flourished. Muslims, followers of the religion of Islam, worship Allah, the One True God who "knoweth all things." Buddhists speak of finding spiritual fulfillment in "the truth," and so do members of such other Far Eastern systems of belief as Confucianism, Taoism and Shintoism.

But there is deception as well as truth in the world, and religious teaching must contend with that reality. That is where the idea of Satan or the devil comes in. As God represents truth, so Satan represents falsehood. In fact, the very word "devil" comes from the ancient Greek word *"diabolos,"* meaning "slanderer," one who spreads malicious false reports.

The idea of the deceitful evil that challenges the goodness and truth of God is widespread in religious belief. It was Satan, in the guise of a serpent, who is traditionally credited with having spoken the first lie in the Garden of Eden. It was of "your father the devil" that Jesus warned the unbelievers at the Mount of Olives. "When he [the devil] speaketh a lie," Jesus said, "he speaketh of his own: for he is a liar, and the father of it." Muslims believe in evil beings or *jinn* (origin of the English word "genies"), embodiments of darkness and deception, as Allah is of light and truth. In the religions of the Far East, which tend more toward mysticism than do Islam, Christianity or Judaism, it is disorder and chaos, a kind of disharmony or dishonesty in the universe, that stand opposed to the ultimate reality of nature and the Supreme Being.

All religions, each in its own way, require their faithful to reject the darkness, confusion and deceit of evil and the devil, and to strive toward God's truth. Of course, the kind of truth associated with a Supreme Being is abstract and awesome, something beyond the comprehension of mortal men and women. But men and women can, religion teaches, approach that truth and try to exemplify it on a human level in their daily lives. Every religion gives its followers certain rules for accomplishing both.

For the mystical religions of the East, the rules tend to be nonspecific. Typically, they call for meditation and other spiritual means of bringing oneself into a sense of harmony and repose with nature and with the truth and reality that underlie it. Still, a few definite guidelines for human conduct are laid out as well. "Hold faithfulness and sincerity as first principles," Confucius wrote in his *Analects,* and, "When you know a thing, to hold that you know it; and when you do not know a thing, to allow that you do not know it — this is knowledge."

To Muslims, the injunction to truthfulness is more directly aimed at promoting honesty among human beings. "Do not veil the truth with falsehood," says the Koran, the holy book of Islam, "nor conceal the truth knowingly."

Christians and Jews find the rules even more specifically geared to day-to-day living. "Thou shalt not bear false witness against thy neighbor," God told Moses on Mount Sinai. That is the ninth of the Ten Commandments, and the only one that explicitly prohibits a lie of a particular type. Several other of the commandments, however, do relate to honest dealing. The seventh forbids adultery and the eighth, stealing, both of which could be presumed to entail deceit. Killing, prohibited by the fifth commandment, could involve it as well, and so might covetousness — the longing for something that belongs to another — the subject of the last of the commandments. The first, of course, "Thou shalt have no other gods before me," warns against the ultimate lie — denying the one truth that is God himself.

Elsewhere in the Bible we read of humankind's inclination toward falsehood and of God's abhorrence of it. The Old Testament prophet Zechariah records God's words to him: "Speak ye every man the truth to his neighbor; execute the judgment of truth and peace in your gates . . . love no false oath." Another prophet, Jeremiah, lamented the wickedness of his people. "They bend their tongues like their bows for lies: but they are not valiant for the truth . . . for they proceed from evil to evil. . . ." The psalmist asked, "Lord, who shall abide in thy tabernacle?" and answered his own question: "He that . . . speaketh the truth."

As for what happens to those who do not speak truly, the New Testament story of Ananias and Sapphira affords a terrible lesson. Ananias — his name was to become synonymous with "liar" — and Sapphira were among the earliest converts to Christianity. After Jesus' death, the disciple Peter urged the couple to sell a parcel of land and give the proceeds to the church.

Ananias and Sapphira made the sale but secretly conspired to keep back some of the money for themselves. "Why hath Satan filled thine heart to lie?" Peter demanded. "Thou hast not lied unto men, but unto God." God's judgment was swift. Ananias was struck dead and so was his wife, punished not so much for greed as for the deception the two had plotted. "And great fear came upon all the church," the story ends, "and upon as many as heard these things." The fear lingers still today. For everyone brought up in the Judeo-Christian tradition — even for those who may not be particularly religious — there remains the sense that lying is wrong and the uneasy conviction that retribution follows surely upon deceit.

Yet — and here's the contradiction again — people do lie. They lie despite their fear of punishment and despite the teachings of religion. Sometimes, when they lie to achieve a purely selfish goal, such as winning a promotion or hiding a guilty secret, they may feel ashamed of what they have done. But at other times, as in the case of a patriot who lies to serve her country or of a father who lies to save his child, they feel positively heroic about it. For human beings have devised elaborate methods of distinguishing among lies and of rating them according to various scales of moral values. They have learned to label some lies "good" and some "bad," and even found means of convincing themselves and others that a lie can be more true than the truth. These means and methods make up the second way in which people have sought to reconcile the conflict they see between the need to lie and the need for truth. The distinguishing, rating and moral labeling have become the work of philosophy; of ethicists, moralists and theologians who ponder the principles of universal right and truth and speculate about how those principles apply to ordinary life and living.

To some philosophers, the principles have appeared to be absolute and unbending. Immanuel Kant, the eighteenth-century German thinker, was one of them. Kant believed that all lies are immoral. No matter what a person's reason for lying, and no matter how beneficial a lie might be, it is impossible to justify any deception, according to him. "Truthfulness is a duty which must be regarded as the ground of all duties," he wrote. To dramatize his point, Kant posed this question: Is it right to lie to a would-be murderer who demands to know where his intended victim has taken refuge?

"No" was Kant's answer. Why not? Because, "if by telling a lie you have prevented murder, you have made yourself . . . responsible for all the consequences."

The consequences could be unexpected, Kant warned. To put the murderer off the track, you have told him that the person he is looking for is not at home. That is a lie — but what if it turns into the truth? Suppose the victim did go home, then slipped out again, hoping to avoid his enemy that way? "If the murderer had then met him as he went away and murdered him, you might justly be accused as the cause of his death" Kant wrote.

Kant's position seems extreme, but he was willing to go further. Even if your lie did save a life, he maintained, it would still be immoral. That is because every lie told constitutes an attack upon that fundamental truthfulness that is essential to human society. *Any* lie inflicts damage upon people as a whole, however helpful it may be to one individual. "For a lie always harms another; if not some other particular man, still it harms mankind generally."

Other clerics and thinkers have been less rigid. St. Augustine and St. Thomas Aquinas, both theologians of the Roman Catholic church, also regarded all lies as wrong and sinful. Unlike Kant, though, they conceded that some types of lies may be thought of as less sinful than others.

St. Augustine, born in the fourth century A.D., discussed the subject of human deception in a treatise entitled "Lying." In it, he organized lies into eight separate moral categories. The first — and in Augustine's view the worst — category consisted of lies "uttered in the teaching of religion." Pretending to agree with a heresy, a belief that runs counter to official church teaching, in order to uncover heretics within a congregation, would be an example of such a lie. Even though Augustine believed that heretics endanger their immortal souls, locating and correcting them through deception seemed sinful to him.

The second-worst type of lie, in Augustine's scheme of things, is one that injures someone unjustly. Then come those that harm one person while helping another, then "the lie which is told solely for the pleasure of lying," and so on. Least serious of all is a lie that protects someone and harms no one else. Although Augustine could not bring himself to say that a lie even in this eighth category could be considered right, neither could he say that it would be as immoral as one in the first.

St. Augustine also tackled the matter of white lies, lies put forth for the purpose of sparing the feelings of someone who might be hurt in some way if he or she was forced to hear the truth. He proposed this situation: a desperately ill man, unaware that his beloved only son has died, asks how the boy is. If the father learns the truth, it may kill him.

Naturally, it would be wrong to assure the father that his son is well or to say "I don't know how he is." Augustine made plain his belief that the only really right course would be absolute frankness. But his feelings as a man had also to be considered. "Often . . . human sympathy overcomes me," Augustine confessed. For such painful truth telling, he wondered, "who is sufficient?" Yet we ought to make ourselves sufficient, he was convinced, because the habit of lying has a way of growing. Bit by bit well-meant little white lies can add up to a mountain of big serious deceptions. Therefore, he concluded, "it is not true that sometimes we ought to lie." Inevitably, however, we sometimes will, and ranking lies on a scale of moral seriousness was the way Augustine chose to help fallible human beings cope with that reality.

St. Thomas Aquinas chose a similar way. Aquinas, who lived in the thirteenth century, also regarded all lies as sins. Like Augustine, however, he was willing to allow that some are less sinful than others. To help people understand the relative evil of their various falsehoods, Aquinas formulated a three-step scheme of his own.

First, Aquinas said, there are officious lies, those uttered with the intention of helping someone — a potential murder victim, perhaps, or a dying man. Second are jocose lies, untruths told to amuse or entertain. Myths, legends and stories about such nonexistent figures as Santa Claus might be examples of this second type of lie. Third are mischievous lies. Only these, which are deliberately intended to take advantage of people or to injure them, amount to mortal sins, for which the soul may be condemned. For, Aquinas wrote, "the sin of lying is diminished if it is directed to some good."

Over the years, other thinkers have adopted this practical way of resolving the contradiction between the necessity for truth and the need to deceive. Desiderius Erasmus, born in Holland in 1466, reasoned that it is simply not possible to stick to the position that all lies are immoral. Erasmus was a priest in the Roman Catholic church, but he was also a humanist, someone with a strong sense of the importance of human interests, values and judgments. Among the hypothetical questions he pondered was this: Would it be moral to tell one harmless lie if doing so would save the souls of all humanity? Erasmus's answer was a firm yes.

Martin Luther's would have been the same. It was Luther, born in Germany in 1483 and a former Catholic priest, who helped lead the Protestant Reformation. Luther disagreed with St. Augustine about the desirability of lies on behalf of religion. "What harm would it do," he asked, "if a man told a good strong lie for the sake of the good and for the Christian Church?" God would not condemn such a deception, he thought.

Others who have written about the ethics of lying have addressed themselves more directly to deception in the everyday world, particularly the everyday world of politics and public life. Sir Francis Bacon, a sixteenth-century English philosopher and statesman, believed that a certain amount of deception is inevitable in government. Perhaps it is even desirable. A "mixture of falsehood," he suggested, "is like allay in coin of gold or silver." An allay (alloy) is a mixture of a base metal like copper or zinc with a precious metal such as gold. Gold alloy is three to five times stronger than pure gold, and unlike the pure substance, able to stand up to rough daily usage. Falsehood in government, Bacon thought, is like the alloy, a necessary evil that "embaseth" the coin yet "may make the metal work the better."

The Dutch-born Hugo Grotius, Bacon's younger contemporary, was similarly pragmatic about the occasional lie. A humanist and a lawyer, Grotius derived his ethical ideas from his legal training and from his sense of the legal and moral rights people ought to enjoy. Lies are wrong, he thought, insofar as they interfere with the rights of those being lied to. Fundamental to those rights is what he called "liberty of judgment." All of us have an inborn right to make up our own mind about matters without having to contend with false information meant to trick us and influence our thinking. For instance, if a witness lies in a court of law with the intention of swaying a jury, that is wrong.

People have a right to expect honesty from everyone with whom they communicate, Grotius went on. His words call to mind the ideas of those in the twentieth century who say that although deception may have played a role in human evolution and in the development of human society and language, deception itself would be impossible without a foundation of truth. Honesty, Grotius thought, "is . . . that mutual obligation which men . . . willed to introduce at the time when they determined to make use of speech and similar signs; for without such an obligation the invention of speech would have been void of result.'' Grotius knew that there is no use in talking or exchanging other signals unless people agree in advance that those signals are to be trustworthy.

However, Grotius also knew that people do — and sometimes must — disregard their obligation to the truth. But when? Why? And with whom? Whose ''liberty of judgment'' might people occasionally be justified in violating? Essentially, Grotius's answer was, anyone who stands to benefit from the deception. A child might benefit from a lie meant to spare his feelings, for instance. Soldiers may fight more valiantly if their leaders assure them that they cannot lose — even when the chances of victory are small. Grotius also considered it permissible to lie to anyone who clearly wants to be deceived, such as sick people eager to hear false reassurances about their health.

Other philosophers have reflected Grotius's ideas, especially his idea that lies are moral if they accomplish public good. Among those who most forcefully advanced this position was an Englishman named Jeremy Bentham. Bentham lived from 1748 to 1832 and was one of the founders of a social philosophy known as Utilitarianism.

Bentham and the Utilitarians rejected the position that lies are immoral because God has said they are.

"Falsehood, take it by itself . . . can . . . never con-stitute any offense at all," Bentham declared. Lies are, in themselves, neutral — neither good nor bad.

In fact, the Utilitarians ruled out moral absolutes al-together. Rather, they believed that words and deeds are to be judged on the basis of their consequences and on how they affect the people of a society. Those that harm people are bad. Those that benefit people are good. Those that benefit more people, or that benefit them to a greater degree, are even better. "The greatest hap-piness of the greatest number" — that was the Utili-tarians' motto. From their point of view, a lie that helps a hundred people would be more worthy than one that helps only fifty. A lie that turns out to be good for fifty people is more valuable than a truth that is good for ten. Above all, it is up to mortal men and women, not God, to make the judgments about each particular lie. It is up to them to weigh the consequences of a false-hood and to decide whether or not it was worth the telling.

In this century, too, philosophers have turned their attention to issues of truth and deception. One who did was Dietrich Bonhoeffer, born in Germany in 1906. For Bonhoeffer, being truthful meant, first and fore-most, being truthful before God. Bonhoeffer, a Prot-estant minister and theologian, believed that if a person was truthful in this way, he or she could be justified in lying to other human beings for certain reasons. To illustrate his point, Bonhoeffer used the example of a boy whose teacher asks, in front of the class, whether it is true that his father comes home drunk at night.

As a matter of fact, it is true. The boy knows it. But he knows something else as well, something of far greater significance. He knows that he loves his family and that it is important to him. That love and importance constitute truths of their own, truths more fundamental than the trivial truth his teacher is demanding to hear. But the boy is not skillful enough with words to be able to express a thought that complex, and so he lies. He preserves the large truth that is his family by resorting to a smaller falsehood about one member of that family. No, he says, his father does not come home drunk.

"The child acted correctly," Bonhoeffer wrote, because his lie contained more of the real truth — the kind of truth that God recognizes — than a literally true answer would have. It was a lie put forth in the service of truth. Sometimes, Bonhoeffer believed, lies must be told so that more vital truths can be preserved.

It was that way for Pastor Bonhoeffer himself. By the early 1930s, when Bonhoeffer was in his twenties, a man named Adolf Hitler was coming to power in Germany. Hitler was a founder of that country's Nazi party and its leading member. He was also a master liar, as he himself boasted. In his book *Mein Kampf*, a work that combined autobiography with political and social theory, Hitler vigorously advocated lying as a means of achieving public goals. In fact, from a politician's point of view, the bigger a lie was the better, he wrote, since "the great masses of the people . . . will more easily fall victims to a great lie than to a small one."

Hitler practiced what he preached and his lies were great indeed. With the help of a tight circle of associates, including his propaganda chief, Joseph Goebbels, he assured Germans that they were superior to members of all other races and destined to dominate world affairs. True, Germany was in dire social, political and economic straits in the 1930s. Its problems, Hitler and Goebbels said, had all begun in 1918, when World War I ended. In November of that year, the German army had been forced to surrender to the Allied forces of England, France, the United States and a number of other countries. But that surrender had not come about because Germany had been defeated on the battlefield, Hitler and his cohorts maintained. Rather, it was the work of a small group of German politicians and businessmen who had been eager to see the war end so they could get back to making money. It was these men who had caused their nation's downfall with a traitorous "stab in the back." Although the Nazis did not invent the stab-in-the-back theory, they were the ones promoting it most strongly in the Germany of the early thirties.

The theory was untrue. The German army had been thoroughly beaten in World War I. A great many Germans, however, bearing out Hitler's contention that big lies are easily swallowed, clutched enthusiastically at the false account of the events of 1918. Many also accepted the Nazi insistence that it was *Jewish* politicians and financiers in particular who had engineered the German surrender. And those Germans adopted the Nazi position that it was Jews who were to blame for the terrible economic suffering that Germany, and much of the rest of the world, had been undergoing since the Great Depression began in 1929.

Upon such lies as these, Hitler rose to the head of the German government. Early in 1933 he became the nation's chancellor and, soon after that, the Führer, the Leader — absolute dictator. On his orders, his political opponents were imprisoned, tortured and murdered. Armed members of his special elite forces were given license to terrorize the populace, especially the Jewish populace. Brown-clad troopers roamed the streets, smashing into Jewish homes and shops, wrecking them and killing their owners or dragging them off to extermination or concentration camps. Over the next twelve years, more than six million European Jews were to die at Nazi hands. Before their death, many were employed as slave labor or subjected to hideously cruel medical "experiments." Catholics and Protestants who criticized the regime found themselves hauled off to the camps as well. So did Gypsies, homosexuals, scholars and thousands upon thousands of others. By the late 1930s, Hitler had mobilized Germany's army and World War II began in the final year of the decade. It was to last until just after the Führer's suicide in April 1945.

By then Bonhoeffer was dead, too, hanged in a German prison on April 9, 1945. He had been arrested two years earlier and accused of being part of a plot to overthrow Hitler. It was not a false charge; the young minister believed that he had a moral duty to act against so great an evil as Hitler.

This self-imposed duty ensnared Bonhoeffer in a web of human deceit. For the sake of the plot, lies had to be told and deceptions carried out. Bonhoeffer assumed a false identity, disguised himself and once traveled to Sweden on forged papers. But through it all, he remained convinced that his lies were entirely ethical. Like the child who lies to his teacher about his father's drinking, Bonhoeffer conceived his deceptions in pursuit of a higher truth, the truth that God would recognize, the truth that the Nazis were so monstrous, so immoral, that lies were justified if those lies were aimed at driving them out of power.

Few philosophers have had to put their moral convictions regarding truth and deception to the test in the way Dietrich Bonhoeffer did. Few of us, we hope, will have to either. But smaller dilemmas of right and wrong, of truth and falsehood, do confront us, and frequently. They confront other people as well, people in business, education, sports, politics and every other walk of life. Can the ideas of philosophy and the teachings of religion help them — and us — to resolve those dilemmas?

4
Who Lies? What Happens?

Dietrich Bonhoeffer lived and died in the belief that the deceptions he practiced in the plot against Adolf Hitler were morally correct. God would count those deceptions not as sins but as acts of virtue, he was sure.

Not everyone would share his conviction. Immanuel Kant, for one, believed that all lies are wrong under all circumstances. In his view, it would be wrong to lie to a potential murderer about his intended victim's whereabouts, even if the falsehood saved a life. Deceiving people who had murdered, and who had committed other crimes and atrocities, was exactly what Bonhoeffer and his fellow conspirators were attempting to do.

Those who, like Kant, believe that the truth is so sacred and so essential that no cause can ever justify straying from it set a high standard for the rest of us to try to live up to. Yet it is also a simple standard. Taken literally, it leaves no room at all for doubt or confusion. If every lie is wrong, then every liar is equally at fault. There is no need to ask questions or engage in ethical debate. No one has to wonder whether or not it would be right to lie in this situation or for that reason. No one needs to consider how bad a particular deception might be. To lie is to sin and that is that. Telling a white lie to comfort a friend must be as wicked as falsely accusing that same friend of a crime. Bonhoeffer's deceptions must be as immoral as Hitler's.

That would be a tough proposition for most of us to accept. No matter how highly a person values truth, he or she is bound to have trouble equating comfort with false accusations, or Dietrich Bonhoeffer with Adolf Hitler. Most philosophers and theologians, however moral or religious, have had to agree that all lies are not equal. Some, Bonhoeffer and Bentham among them, have gone further, asserting that in some situations, telling a lie can be more ethical than sticking to the truth.

But if some lies are very bad, some not so bad, and some acceptable or even admirable, how can we sort them out? How can we measure their worth — or wickedness?

For Bonhoeffer, the measure of a lie rested in the motive behind it. As long as a person's reason for telling a lie is good — meaning that he or she is acting out of a desire to remain in harmony with the truth that

God recognizes — the deception is ethical, Bonhoeffer believed. We will look at this idea in more detail in chapter 5.

Other thinkers have chosen to look at deception from slightly different perspectives. To some, the way to judge a lie seems to be to look at what actually happens as a result of that lie, rather than at what the liar hopes will happen, or intends to have happen. St. Augustine was among those who sought to rate the morality of a deception primarily according to the effect it had. In his view, a lie that helps one person while harming another is better than one that injures someone unjustly while not helping anyone else. Francis Bacon also regarded a lie's consequence as essential to measuring its worth. So did Jeremy Bentham. In fact, few people have surpassed Bentham and his nineteenth-century Utilitarian colleagues in their enthusiasm for judging a lie's morality by its results. For them, consequence was all, and lies had no ethical value apart from what they accomplished for good or ill.

Still another philosophical approach to sorting out lies is to consider the type of people involved in a deception. Those who look at lies from this point of view believe that the nature of the relationship between the liar and the lied-to, and the kind of responsibility one has toward the other, provides an important basis for deciding whether or not a particular lie is ethical.

Of those thinkers whose ideas we examined in the

previous chapter, the one who applied himself most directly to the "who" of deception was the lawyer Hugo Grotius. As we saw, Grotius believed that it is ethical to lie to anyone who needs, or wants, to be shielded from the truth — children, for example. His rationale: such people lack, for one reason or another, the right to that liberty of judgment that human beings ordinarily enjoy.

Do they? Most people probably would agree that children lack it, to an extent, anyway. "Don't worry about Aunt Susan," a mother tells her five-year-old. "She'll be fine." Actually, she won't be; Susan's doctor has diagnosed a terminal illness. But the mother believes a five-year-old is too young to face such devastating news all at once. Slowly and carefully, she will introduce the little girl to the idea of illness and death. By the time her aunt passes away, the child will understand.

Most people might regard that as the wisest and most loving way to handle this situation. But what about the mother who assures a toddler that "it won't hurt a bit" as the doctor prepares to give him a shot? Do all children lack all liberty of judgment all the time?

That question suggests others. Our society, unlike Grotius's, looks upon teenagers as children, or rather, as people who are somewhat less than fully adult. Does that mean they may be lied to as freely as young children may be? What about youngsters who are especially emotionally mature or intellectually precocious for their age? Do they have a greater right to truth than their more average brothers and sisters?

What subjects are appropriate for lies? Some adults feel justified in deceiving children about important things like illness and death. Others lie about private family matters such as alcoholism, divorce, incest or illegitimate births. Still others limit their fibs to trivia, telling fantastic tales about Santa Claus, the Easter bunny and the tooth fairy. And children frequently hear warnings in the form of lies. Parents, teachers, the police and others may try to impress them with the dangers of talking to strangers, or accepting rides from them, by recounting exaggerated or made-up accounts of kidnapped or murdered children, for example. That is their right, the adults reason, as people who are older, wiser and more knowledgeable about the ways of the world than those they seek to protect.

Adults may even believe that their superior age gives them the right to employ deception to teach a moral lesson. In 1800, an American parson named Mason Locke Weems wrote a children's book with an unusually cumbersome title: *The Life of George Washington: With Curious Anecdotes, Equally Honorable to Himself and Exemplary to His Young Countrymen.* One of the "curious anecdotes" he related told how the boy George chopped down a cherry tree and — "with the sweet face of youth brightened with the inexpressible charm of all-conquering truth'' — resisted the temptation to lie about what he had done. Questionable as Weems's writing style may have been, his facts were even more so. The cherry tree story was completely his own invention. Yet, as an adult instructing children, he felt quite comfortable telling it. Many adults today feel the same way.

If children may be lied to, who should decide whether or not a lie is appropriate in a particular situation? Parents? Other relatives? Baby sitters and family friends? Teachers? Religious instructors? And once the decision to lie has been made, which adults are entitled to carry it out?

Finally, what about fairness? Children are born trusting, capable of believing the most far-fetched of tales. Is it fair to take advantage of that trust? Consider this, too: if there is one thing grown-ups demand of children, it is honesty. Is it right for adults to deny them the truth in return?

Questions like these have no hard-and-fast answers. Certainly, most adults are going to feel obliged to lie to some children at some times. But the questions do suggest that there must be limits to the idea that it is all right for any grown-up to lie to any child just because one is older than the other.

Grotius also considered it acceptable to lie to anyone who wants to be deceived or who does not take care to make sure he or she will not be. Unlike children, such people cannot be said to lack liberty of judgment. Rather, they choose not to employ it. That choice makes them partners in their own deception and the accomplices of those who seek to defraud or mislead them.

All of us know what it is like to be in this position. Self-deception is among the commonest of human failings. Who hasn't been pleased by compliments that he or she knows are exaggerated or undeserved? All of us have gone along with others' phony excuses from time to time in order to save face or avoid having our feelings hurt.

We cooperate in our own deception in other ways, as well. One entire industry — the advertising industry — is in large part a tribute to the willingness of human beings to allow themselves to be fooled. People spend millions of dollars every year on products that promise to get clothes "whiter than white," or "brighter than bright," for example. Whiter than white does not exist. A dental rinse that "reduces plaque on teeth by over 300 percent" would have to take all the plaque off a user's teeth, take it off again, then take it off a third time in order to do the job claimed for it. Yet Americans buy the product. They buy other products of dubious value: anti-aging skin creams, "germ-killing" mouthwashes, hair restorers, diet pills — the list could go on and on.

People also deceive themselves — and allow themselves to be lied to — about more profound matters. The dying may cling to false assurances about the seriousness of their condition and their prospects for recovery. Parents ignore the warning signs that tell of a son's drug habit and gratefully accept his word for it that he's "clean." People are attracted to religious cults or television evangelists and fall victim to self-proclaimed holy men and women who use the cult or the broadcast to win power and to enrich themselves from the offerings of believers.

Is there anything wrong with that? If people are pleased to join a cult or to be manipulated by greedy preachers, why stop them? If they don't want to face a difficult truth, why should they have to? If they choose to believe all that they see and hear in commercials, or allow themselves to be soothed with insincere compliments and excuses, that is their business, too.

The argument goes further. If people want to be deceived, it continues, then there can be nothing morally wrong with anyone else's cooperating in that deception. If consumers want to put their faith in valueless products, then it is okay to manufacture, advertise and sell those products. If some people cannot deal with reality and look for false assurances instead, then it is morally acceptable for others to offer those assurances. If they find genuine comfort in a fraudulent religion, then how can it be said that those who provide that comfort are doing anything unscrupulous? There can be nothing unethical about lying to a person who is obviously hoping you will do just that.

There is another type of human relationship that serves to justify lying as well, Grotius believed. This is the relationship between the governed and the governing. Just as adults can be assumed to be wiser than children and to have better judgment than they do, men and women who hold positions of authority may be presumed to know more about what is good for the public than the public itself knows. That superior knowledge gives government officials rights over ordinary citizens, and permits those officials to deceive the people on occasion.

Many in the world today would agree. Sheriff Frank Hackett, for example, made it clear that he did when he talked to news reporters about the television sting operation we looked at in chapter 1. As sheriff, Hackett had certain rights that others in Kennebec County lacked. He and his deputies were legally superior to the men and women they sought to trap: they were public officials who had been granted specific responsibility to enforce the law. What was more, their sting operation was not directed against all the county's population but only against a small number of those who had been accused of breaking the law and of having tried to evade the consequences. Lawbreaking usually involves a degree of dishonesty, and those who have

committed crimes are generally assumed to have for-
feited at least a portion of their right to receive honest
treatment from others. Stings like Hackett's have been
declared legal in the courts and are becoming increasingly routine at all levels of government — federal, state,
county and local. Most Americans find them acceptable, although it is important to remember that the men
and women targeted in such operations may only have
been accused of criminal activity, not convicted of it.

People seem further to agree that law enforcement
agencies are justified in engaging in other forms of
deception. The police practice of patrolling highways
in unmarked vehicles in order to catch speeders is
one deception we have all learned to live with. Others include the setting of traps to catch drunk drivers,
the staking out of stores or businesses in anticipa-
tion of attempts at robbery and the disguising of
police officers as prostitutes or potential mugging victims.

The police are not the only public officials who believe that their responsibilities and the superior positions they hold permit them to use deception as a tool
to reach certain of their goals. There are those throughout government who believe the same. This belief is
one reason Americans read and hear so much about
lying on the part of their elected and appointed officials.

Often, the lies concern money. The reason for this

is simple: every agency of government must go to the U.S. Congress (or to state, county or local lawmaking bodies) to get the funds to carry out its work. If lawmakers can be convinced that the work is important and urgent, the agency will get the money. And the more urgent and important the work seems, the more money will be forthcoming.

The work of government *is* urgent and important. It is urgent and important in the U.S. Department of Defense (DOD), for instance, and everyone in the department knows it. But department members also know that Congress and the American people may not be as aware of the urgency and importance as they are. DOD is charged with seeing to it that the U.S. military is strong, its services well equipped, its weaponry up to date and its officers and enlisted men and women properly paid and cared for. Achieving all that costs money — billions of dollars every year. Sometimes, though, Congress balks at spending so much. Can't some of the money that DOD wants be spent closer to home, Congress asks, on education, medical care for the needy and elderly, job-training programs and the like? No, says DOD, the military needs money more than the poor and unemployed do. As one way of proving their point, department officials publish yearly comparisons of the defense outlays of this country and the Soviet Union. The officials know exactly how much the United States spends, of course, but in the case of the Soviets, hard figures are unavailable. Estimates must do. But estimates cover a wide range — anywhere from five to seven billion dollars for this new weapon, or fifteen to nineteen billion for that one. In each case, says Franklyn D. Holzman, professor of economics at Tufts University and a DOD critic, defense officials settle on the highest possible figure. That allows them to come up with misleading comparisons that demonstrate how far this country "lags" behind the Soviet Union in military spending.

Nor are dollar amounts the only numbers subject to manipulation by some of those responsible for governing the nation. In the mid-1980s, Americans became aware of the problem of children who are kidnapped or who disappear in other ways. Representatives of the federal government's National Center for Missing and Exploited Children explained the urgency of the problem to Congress. According to them, one and a half million American youngsters under age thirteen vanish every year. Alarmed, Congress voted to fund the center generously. Soon after, though, Americans began hearing that the missing-child figures had been greatly inflated. About thirty thousand children disappear each year, experts now say, most of them snatched by a divorced parent who has lost a child custody suit.

Suppressing information is another form of deception and this, too, can be an instrument for establishing public policy. In the early 1980s, British transportation authorities commissioned a study to find out what would happen to the nation's traffic death rate if the wearing of automobile seat belts by drivers and their front-seat passengers was made mandatory. According to those who conducted the study, deaths among strapped-in riders would fall, while those among pedestrians and bicyclists would rise. The reason: drivers, knowing that they and their passengers were protected, would unconsciously tend to take more chances and to operate a little less carefully than before. Transportation officials kept silent about the report's unsettling finding, and the seat belt rule went into effect in February 1983. Over the next twenty months, driver and passenger deaths were down; pedestrian and biker fatalities, sharply up.

Deception of the public by the government, and of one part of government by another, is almost routine in this country and elsewhere. Congress expects the DOD to overstate its budget needs, for instance. And DOD does — by enough so that even if Congress pares its requests down, the department will still be amply funded. It's almost like a ritual, or a game with unwritten rules.

In wartime, though, deception is anything but a game. It is a weapon in a life-and-death struggle, a technique of survival not entirely unlike an animal's use of deception in the hunt for food. Few rules hold in the heat of battle, and military and civilian leaders generally feel justified in telling any lie that advances their cause and injures the enemy.

The silent lies of censorship are among the most common of wartime deceptions. Battle plans are kept secret from all but a very few. When soldiers write letters home, those letters may be censored to prevent any news of troop movements from leaking out — and into enemy ears. Or the lies may be more direct. Generals may deceive those departing for the front about their exact destination so that they will not let vital information slip, even by accident.

Wartime deception must be as old as human warfare itself. Ancient myths tell how, over three thousand years ago, the Greeks unleashed a mighty attack on Troy, a city in what is now Turkey. After nine years of vainly trying to break through Troy's high defensive walls, the Greeks appeared to give up. They piled into their ships and weighed anchor, leaving behind a gift — a huge wooden horse. Troy's prophet-priest Laocoön warned his people to leave the horse alone. "I fear the Greeks when they come bearing gifts," he told them. But the heedless Trojans ignored his words and dragged the creature behind their walls. Late that night, a few Greek soldiers crept out of its hollow belly and threw open the city gates. In poured their countrymen, who had only pretended to sail away. Troy was captured and destroyed.

The story of the Trojan horse is just a story, but

other wartime deceptions have been real enough. One occurred during World War II, as the Allied forces of England, France and the United States prepared for the invasion of Nazi-occupied Europe. The Allied plan was to set the first troops ashore on the Italian island of Sicily, and to keep that plan a secret, members of a British espionage unit constructed the intricate hoax of "the man who never was." They obtained a body — that of a Scotsman whose father had given permission for its use — and dressed it in a British uniform. In its pockets they planted papers that outlined plans for an Allied landing on Sardinia, an island to the north of Sicily. The British left the body floating off the Spanish coast, where — as they had hoped — it was found by German spies. The Germans retrieved the papers and sent them to their intelligence headquarters in Berlin. When British and American troops landed in Sicily a few weeks later, it was much to the surprise of the German and Italian forces waiting for them miles away on Sardinia.

Propaganda is another form of wartime deception. During World War I, which began in 1914, British propaganda experts spread false reports of terrible atrocities committed by German soldiers in the areas they had occupied. A few of the allegations were that the soldiers had raped dozens of Roman Catholic nuns, cut the hands off countless children and made a sport of tossing babies into the air and catching them on their bayonets. It was true that German rule was harsh in the conquered lands, but these stories were almost entirely without foundation. They did, however, serve to inflame public opinion and stiffen Allied resolve to defeat the "barbarous Hun."

Nor have U.S. leaders hesitated to lie to their own people in time of war. The World War I "atrocity" stories were circulated here, too. Twenty-five years later, in the midst of World War II, American officials perpetrated a different type of deception on the country. Government spokespeople urged citizens to organize drives to collect scrap metal and turn it in to centers set up for the purpose. Ostensibly, the metal was needed for new tanks, jeeps and weapons, but in truth, U.S. manufacturers had little use for the stuff. The "need" for scrap was fabricated by government officials aware of their responsibility to spur patriotic fervor and to make the American people feel they were contributing to the war effort.

Official deception was also a part of this nation's Vietnam War experience. That Southeast Asian conflict began in the 1950s and involved the noncommunist government of South Vietnam on one side and South Vietnamese rebels, backed by communist North Vietnam, on the other. The United States supported the South Vietnamese government; first, in the fifties, with money, weapons and military advice, and later, from the mid-1960s on, with combat troops. Before the fighting stopped ten years later, nearly nine million Americans had served in Vietnam. Over fifty-five thousand had died.

Many of the lies told during the war were similar to the lies of earlier conflicts. Censorship, deceptive military tactics, spying and the double-dealing of secret agents, propagandistic stories of communist atrocities — all were part of the picture. But the Vietnam War was to become distinguished for more elaborate deceptions as well.

As a matter of fact, it was largely through lies that this country got into the fighting to begin with. In the 1950s, the administration of President Dwight D. Eisenhower suppressed certain U.S. intelligence reports about the politics of Southeast Asia. Those reports indicated that about 80 percent of the South Vietnamese population favored unification with the North even if that would mean living under a communist government. But Eisenhower and his advisors, convinced of their duty to halt the spread of communism, kept silent about the reports. Their silence helped set the stage for the United States to go to war to "save" a people from a fate most of them actually wanted.

A decade later, it was the administration of President Lyndon B. Johnson that was being untruthful about Vietnam. In August 1964, Johnson told Congress that North Vietnam had fired on a U.S. ship sailing in international waters thirty miles off its coast. Angry legislators authorized Johnson to take "all necessary measures" to protect American lives and shipping in the area. Johnson did, and from that moment on, America became ever more deeply involved in the fighting. It was years before Congress and the public learned that the "attack" had not been as Johnson depicted it. The U.S. ship was a bare thirteen miles off North Vietnam at the time it occurred. Its captain had been under orders to provoke the incident — thus giving this country an excuse to enter the war. Like Eisenhower, Johnson saw himself as a U.S. president with a responsibility to fight communism.

Other Vietnam War lies were more subtle. To demonstrate American popularity in South Vietnam, U.S. officials arranged village celebrations and invited reporters to take pictures and write stories about them. Other "photo opportunities" included staged scenes of children studying in schools built with American money and of American soldiers handing out gifts to smiling peasants. When the reporters left, the celebrations broke up and the classrooms emptied. The villagers went back to war.

As the months passed, photographers and reporters came to recognize how they were being used to promote the deceptions. Television anchorman Walter Cronkite of CBS-TV, for instance, first visited Vietnam in 1965. The reports he broadcast then were, as he later acknowledged, faithful echoes of the official

U.S. picture of how the war was going. Preparing for a return trip three years later, Cronkite warned CBS executives that things were going to be different from then on. "This time let's say what I think about it," he said.

Cronkite did say what he thought and so did other journalists. Gradually, the American people learned the facts. The United States was not winning the war. Most South Vietnamese were sick of fighting and still hoped for reunification with the North. In the end, they got their wish. The United States withdrew from Vietnam in 1974, leaving behind a single — communist — nation.

Long before that happened, Lyndon Johnson had departed from the White House. Although he could have run for another term of office in 1968, Johnson chose not to. He knew that the war, and the deceptions that had helped fuel it, had left him so unpopular that he had little chance of winning. The 1968 election went to Richard Nixon, who had earlier served as Eisenhower's vice president. Four years later, Nixon was re-elected.

Nixon's second election victory came by a large majority, but it was a triumph that was to cost him dearly. And all because he lied.

The lies for which Nixon was to become notorious began in June 1972, five months before the election. Early on the morning of June 17, seven men were arrested in Washington, D.C., in connection with a break-in at that city's Watergate office complex. Police found five of the seven inside the Watergate offices of the national headquarters of the Democratic political party. The men were stealing files and photographing documents there.

Who would want to spy on the Democrats? The likeliest answer seemed to be: members of the nation's other major political party, the Republican party. President Nixon was a Republican.

Did Nixon or anyone else at the White House know anything about the break-in? That was the next question. Nixon answered it with an unequivocal no.

Most Americans believed him. Nixon enjoyed his landslide victory and embarked upon his second term of office. But the Watergate questions wouldn't go away. Reporters and others began uncovering links between the burglars and people in the White House and in the leadership of the Republican party. They discovered evidence that Nixon and some of those working with him had authorized further illegal activities: other break-ins, the placing of wiretaps on the telephones of political opponents and so on. As the months passed, a few of his aides and advisors began confessing their own lawlessness. A number stepped down from office and a few went to prison.

The president, though, continued to claim that he personally had done nothing wrong. Ordered by the federal courts to turn over documents and other evidence that would show whether or not he was telling the truth, Nixon refused. As president, he said, he had special privileges — executive privilege, he called it — that permitted him to keep those documents to himself even if doing so meant disobeying a court order and concealing information from the public. Clearly, Nixon would have agreed with the lawyer Grotius that national leaders have rights denied to ordinary citizens — including the right to lie. His own lawyer agreed with Grotius, too.   When it comes to the president, the law "has to be applied in different way," Nixon's attorney told the courts, arguing that the president could not be made to surrender evidence that would reveal the truth.

The U.S. Supreme Court — the nation's highest court — disagreed, and told Nixon he must release the evidence. It proved beyond a shadow of a doubt that he had known of the Watergate affair from the start and had been lying about it all along. Disgusted, the American people and the Congress demanded Nixon's resignation. Within a week he had become the first U.S. president ever to resign from office.

That meant two presidents in a row had been forced, in one way or another, from office because of the lies they had told. When the 1976 presidential election came around, one candidate, at least, felt obliged to pledge ahead of time that if elected, he would never deviate from the truth. That candidate was Jimmy Carter, the former governor of Georgia. "I'll never lie to you," Carter assured voters over and over. "I'll never mislead you."

Whether or not as a result of that promise, Carter won the election. Was he as honest as he claimed? One reporter put that question directly to his mother, Lillian Carter. Would her son never lie? the reporter demanded. Never, "Miss Lillian," as she was known, replied. Never? the reporter insisted. Never, ever? Finally, Miss Lillian conceded that Carter might occasionally tell a small white lie. Again the reporter persisted. How small? How white? What is a white lie, anyway? Miss Lillian smiled. "Well," she said, "do you remember when you came in and I told you how pretty you looked and how glad I was to see you . . .?"

Americans emerged from the Watergate years and the Vietnam War angry about being lied to by so many of their highest officials. Many expressed cynicism and a growing distrust of their elected and appointed leaders. The national attitude made it plain that people in this country do not believe that public officials have an automatic right to lie simply because they hold positions of authority and responsibility.

Yet Americans *are* willing to accept lies from their leaders on some occasions or under some circumstances. Even after they learned the truth about the atrocity stories of World War I and about the need for scrap metal during World War II, few objected to having been duped. Few pay much attention to the routine exaggerations of DOD and other government agencies. Few — except those caught in them — express indignation over police stings or speed traps.

In some cases, Americans have shown themselves remarkably tolerant of lying on the part of their leaders. Most were well aware that the man who followed Carter in the White House, Ronald Reagan, lied to them often and about a great variety of topics. Once, Reagan mentioned having fought in World War II and referred to having helped liberate a Nazi concentration camp. He had done neither. Reagan, a former actor, spent the war years in Hollywood, making propaganda films.

At other times, Reagan told apocryphal — untrue or inauthentic — stories to illustrate social or political points he wished to make. One was the tale of a welfare recipient who used a government food stamp of a large denomination to buy an inexpensive item in a grocery store. Accepting his change, the man went down the street to a liquor store and spent the cash on a bottle of vodka. It is a fact that some Americans do rely on food stamps to provide themselves with nonfood items, putting their change toward soap, toilet paper, aspirin — even beer and tobacco. Reagan's story of the vodka-buying welfare cheat was patently untrue, however. Grocery store clerks are forbidden by law to hand out more than ninety-nine cents in change for food stamps, and where would anyone find a bottle of vodka for that amount? Nor are clerks supposed to allow customers to use the stamps to make one separate purchase after another, building up a supply of cash that way. But inaccurate as Reagan's story had to have been, few Americans objected to hearing it.

Americans did object, however, to deceptions undertaken by Reagan and some members of his administration in a few of their international dealings. Upon occasion, a White House spokesman named Larry Speakes issued statements that he claimed — deceitfully — came directly from the president. In 1985, for instance, Speakes talked to reporters covering a meeting between Reagan and Soviet leader Mikhail Gorbachev. According to him, Reagan reassured Gorbachev that "the world [is] breathing easier because we are talking here together." It may have been, but the president had never said so. The eloquent words were Speakes' own.

Other Reagan administration deceptions concerned a small number of American citizens who were being held hostage by terrorists in the Middle Eastern nation of Lebanon. During the months of the Americans' captivity, Reagan repeatedly stated that he never had, and never would, bargain with the terrorists for their release. In November 1986, people learned this was a lie. In fact, Reagan had sent negotiators to another Middle Eastern country, Iran, for the precise purpose of bargaining. The negotiators even had the president's okay to sell weapons to the terrorists' Iranian allies in hopes of getting the Iranians to guarantee the hostages' release. The hope was in vain; although two U.S. hostages were set free, other Americans were seized to take their places. Even after the facts of the arms-for-hostages deal were made public, Reagan continued to deny that any such deal had been struck, or even thought of.

Other Reagan administration foreign policy deceptions had to do with Nicaragua, in Central America. Since 1979, that country had had a government friendly to the Soviet Union. From the outset of his first term of office, Reagan was determined to see that government ousted. He therefore offered U.S. military support to Nicaraguan antigovernment rebels known as *contras*. (*"Contra"* is the Spanish word for "against.") Some of the aid was approved by Congress and handed over openly. But much of it was given secretly — and illegally. And members of the Reagan administration lied to the press, to Congress and to the public about having provided it. Some officials also denied — falsely — having known that a great deal of the illegal *contra* aid had been paid for out of the profits of the Iranian arms-for-hostages trade. At first, public opinion was split as to whether or not the president and his aides were right to have lied in each of these cases, but in the end, most Americans came to the conclusion that they had not been.

Why not? Why do people accept one presidential lie and not another? How do they decide that some lies are acceptable or necessary and others unjustified or immoral?

Part of the answer must have to do with whether or not a particular lie affects them in a damaging way. Reagan's food stamp story probably struck most people as harmless enough, since it reflected the fact that some food stamp recipients do indeed cheat. On a deeper level, the story struck a responsive chord with the resentment many Americans feel for welfare recipients in general.

In other cases, too, a lie's effect appears to be harmless, or even beneficial. Some deceptive law enforcement tactics cut down on highway speeding, making the roads safer for all. Others reduce the criminal activities of certain types of lawbreakers, a result any law-abiding citizen would approve.

Similarly, the atrocity stories of World War I and the phony scrap metal drives of World War II seemed to have positive effects. Both helped Americans feel good about standing united behind a worthwhile — and ultimately successful — war effort. The deceptions of the Vietnam War, by contrast, served only to drag this country deeper and deeper into a conflict that destroyed thousands of lives in a losing cause. Little wonder that the public came to condemn those lies, or that it condemned the lies of the Iran-*contra* affair, which exposed the United States to scathing criticism from around the world. It seems to be as St. Augustine said: lies that help someone while harming no one are better than those that injure someone unjustly while not helping anyone else. Augustine may have been right about something else. Maybe people should be looking at a lie's consequences, rather than at its "who," as they attempt to judge its merits.

Rating lies according to their consequences seems an excellent idea, and not just for lies in public life. Take lies told to children. We've already seen how difficult it can be to call those lies right or wrong simply on the basis of *who* is being deceived. But looking at *what happens* when a child is deceived in a specific instance sheds new light on the ethics of that particular deception.

For example, lying to a five-year-old about death has the effect of protecting that child from a reality she is not yet equipped to handle. Isn't that what makes the lie seem right? Telling a fearful child that a doctor's shot won't hurt may also seem to have a beneficial result. The child stops crying and accepts the treatment. But will the consequences of the lie end there? What will the child do when he finds that the shot does hurt? What about the next time he needs an inoculation? How will he react to finding that grown-ups — his own mother among them — are not to be trusted?

The advantage of judging a lie by its consequences is that it allows room for discretion. Rather than saying, "It is all right for adults to deceive children," the statement becomes, "It is all right to deceive children if the deception helps them." It's not a matter of, "It's okay for advertisers and others to lie to those who want to be cajoled into believing what is not true," but, "Helping in another's self-deception is okay if that deception is not harmful." Instead of, "Public officials may lie because they have special privileges," it is, "Officials may lie when the lie truly serves the public." Sorting out lies according to their consequences seems to make sense because it offers the opportunity to line up the good effects alongside the bad, and see how the two compare.

In a few cases, the good effects clearly outweigh the bad ones. A mother's lie to a child about a dying relative may be an example of such a deception. Another example is recounted by Harvard University ethicist Sissela Bok in her book *Lying: Moral Choice in Public and Private Life*. According to Bok, a young woman was traveling in a remote part of Africa when she came upon a village occupied by a group of former head hunters. The villagers invited the traveler to a feast and — mark of special honor — asked her to partake of the tribal delicacy: baby mice dipped in melted butter and swallowed live. As her hosts eyed her expectantly, the woman thought quickly and grasped at a lie. Her religion, she announced regretfully, specifically forbade the eating of live baby mice.

How could anyone condemn such a fib? And how, many ask, could anyone condemn the other white lies that all of us hear — and tell — under far less drastic circumstances every day of our lives? The petty insincerities of unmeant compliments and phony excuses are far too trivial to be counted as unethical, they say. They may even be necessary, serving to make life easier and more agreeable for everyone. "A mixture of a lie doth ever add pleasure," Sir Francis Bacon wrote. He was thinking not just of flattery but of the "deceptions" of fiction and poetry. Others, like the seventeenth-century French playwright Jean Baptiste Molière, have agreed that white lies are essential among civilized people. "Wouldn't the social fabric come undone," one of Molière's characters asks, "if we were wholly frank with everyone?"

Many think so, and social lies abound. But are all of them really as harmless as people like to think they are? St. Augustine would not have said so. The most innocent-seeming of white lies can grow to "a plague . . . [of] huge proportions through small additions," he warned. The plague of consequences can affect both the liar and the lied-to, Augustine might have continued. Making a practice of soliciting or accepting insincerities leaves a person vulnerable to a rude awakening when reality intrudes — as it is sure to do eventually. Making a practice of uttering them can have the effect of turning an honest person into a hypocrite.

Other apparently trivial deceptions may have their darker side, as well. Take advertising. Selling a brand of laundry soap with a "whiter than white" slogan is hardly likely to have dire results. But what about ads that induce the gullible to waste good money on creams "guaranteed" to stop the aging process of human skin or to grow hair on bald heads? What about those that tempt consumers to buy diet pills? Some such pills have been shown to be addictive or to have other adverse health effects. Glossy magazine ads link cigarettes with sophistication, success and outdoor sports. The link is not spelled out in so many words, but it is there in pictures and images. It is a false link, as overwhelming scientific evidence demonstrates. Can the consequences of this falsehood — the American Cancer Society says 300,000 people die in this country every year from smoking-related illnesses — be labeled "trivial" or "harmless"?

What about the consequences of the atrocity propaganda of World War I? On the surface, those lies seem to have been harmless. Yet a closer look reveals something more. The stories aroused violent anti-German feeling. In both England and the United States, that feeling was expressed not just against German soldiers, or even the people of wartime Germany, but against

English and American citizens who had German sur-
names or were of German ancestry. In England, the
Battenberg family — descended from Queen Victoria
and later to produce Philip, the present Duke of
Edinburgh and husband of Queen Elizabeth II — felt
compelled to change its Germanic name to the more
English-sounding Mountbatten. (*"Berg"* is the German word for "mountain.") In this country, German
language and literature courses were dropped from high
school curricula in what was thought of as a patriotic
gesture. German Americans were threatened in the streets
and their homes and places of business vandalized or
attacked by angry mobs.

The consequences of anecdotes like President Reagan's food-stamps-for-vodka story can be serious, too.
That story and others like it helped fan the ill will so
many Americans feel for their fellow citizens who happen to be on welfare. Accepting the president's fiction
as fact made it easier for the nation to accept the deep
cuts his administration made in welfare payments and
in other programs intended to assist the needy. Those
cuts had a devastating effect, not a trivial one, on the
lives of thousands of American men, women and children. The effect was only worsened by the domestic
budget cutting inspired by misleading DOD statistics
regarding United States and Soviet military spending.

Finally, there are those lies whose consequences seem
to be thoroughly bad. Lies about a drug habit are one

example. The silence of British transportation authorities about their seat belt study is another. A third could be the religious lies of fraudulent cult leaders or television evangelists. True, a false religion may offer comfort to a lonely or unhappy person. But what happens when that comfort fades, as it has for so many? Some disillusioned cult members have become severely depressed. A few have committed suicide.

Only a few, though. Many more have survived their disappointment. And some cultists have never suffered any disillusion at all. For them, the deceptions of the false religion continue to offer support. So, some will wonder, can anyone really call the deceptions wrong? Isn't it arguable that the fact that the lies help as many — perhaps more — than they harm make them acceptable? "The greatest happiness of the greatest number," that is the yardstick by which many would judge a lie's morality.

This Utilitarian point of view sounds logical. But it also points up drawbacks to measuring the ethics of a deception simply by its results. One drawback is that it is nearly impossible to decide how much weight to assign to all the consequences of a single lie. Does the suicide of one former cult member outweigh the continued spiritual contentment of ten of the faithful? Of a hundred? What if there are two suicides? How much contentment would be needed to balance that? How should cases of depression be counted in? Would three

be the equivalent of one suicide? Ten depressed people
be more significant than thirty happy ones?

Another problem with judging lies solely according
to their consequences is that the consequences may be
so dissimilar that meaningful comparisons cannot be
drawn. What happens when a family assures a dying
man that he is going to recover his health? On the one
hand, he may enjoy greater peace of mind than he would
have if he had been forced to face the truth. On the
other, the deception could mean that he will neglect to
write a will. He might never get to say good-bye to an
old friend or seek to mend a long-ago quarrel. How
can such different results be compared?

How to compare the contradictory effects of Sheriff
Hackett's sting operation? One effect — the one Hackett emphasized — was that almost two dozen outstanding warrants were wiped off the books. Another, which
Hackett was not so proud of, was the injury inflicted
on William Fullerton, an innocent man and not even
anyone the Sheriff's Department had a reason to be
looking for. Did the injury to Fullerton render the entire deception unjustifiable? Or was Fullerton's emo-
tional hurt the regrettable but minor price that had to
be paid for a novel and successful attempt at law enforcement? Utilitarians would doubtless call it the latter
and justify it with speed and ease. The good — nearly
two dozen wrongdoers brought to justice — out-
weighed the bad — one person injured — Jeremy

Bentham might have said, and that is all a lie need do
to be regarded as ethical. But what would St. Augustine have said? Where would sting operations fit into
his eight-part scheme?

Are consequences alone enough by which to judge a
lie? If so, what would we have to say about Dietrich
Bonhoeffer's lies in pursuit of his anti-Hitler plot? The
consequences of those lies were awful, but not for Hitler. Bonhoeffer and the other conspirators were caught,
imprisoned, treated brutally and eventually executed.
Their plot — and the lies that supported it — did nothing to loosen Hitler's grip on the German nation. If
anything, the Führer acted even more fanatically cruel
after the plot was uncovered than he had before. That
makes it possible to argue that Bonhoeffer's deceptions
actually resulted in more harm than good.

Does that make those deceptions wrong? Surely not.
But the fact that such a question even arises suggests
that just as a lie cannot be judged strictly according to
its "who," neither can it be rated simply by its consequences. Something more is needed: motivation.

5
Lies in a Good Cause

All liars have their reasons for telling the lies they do. Many times, the motive behind a deception is no more than the desire for personal gain. Thieves and cheats, forgers and counterfeiters, plagiarists, dishonest business executives and salespeople, con artists — all employ deception to a greater or lesser degree as they seek to benefit themselves financially.

Other self-serving liars pursue a different type of gain. Richard Nixon deceived the American people about his administration's role in the Watergate cover-up and in other illegal activities not out of money motives but from the determination to preserve his prestige and political power. As the Watergate scandal unfolded, the president allowed one after another of his aides and advisors, some of whom had served him loyally for years, to admit to having done wrong and to having lied about it. The admissions led to disgrace for many, to prison for some. But for more than two years, Nixon's lies permitted him personally to cling to office. Not until the whole truth was finally revealed, in August 1974, did people understand the extent of his lies and the selfish motives that appeared to be behind them. With that understanding came outrage.

No wonder. Nearly everyone agrees that lies designed to serve the liar at the expense of others are wrong. The lie the Old Testament Jacob told his father, Isaac, in order to win the blessing meant for Esau was such a lie. So was the explanation Adam gave God about how he came to eat the forbidden fruit.

Even self-serving lies that do not harm others directly seem wrong to most. Such a lie came in 1984 from an American author named Timothy J. Cooney. Cooney submitted to a publisher a manuscript for a book and, along with it, an enthusiastic letter bearing the signature of Robert Nozick, chairman of the philosophy department at Harvard University. Cooney was "an extremely original thinker," the letter said, and his book, "truly brilliant." The letter did its job; the editor accepted the manuscript and began working toward publication. But when he asked Nozick to write an introduction for the book he so admired, the editor was surprised to learn that the professor had never heard of it — nor of the letter, either. Cooney had — to the amusement of many in the publishing world — written the letter himself. Editorial amusement was heightened by the fact that Cooney's manuscript dealt with the subject of ethics. He had called it *Telling Right from Wrong*.

But if an ethicist like Cooney had trouble distinguishing right from wrong, others have found it easier. St. Augustine assigned selfish and self-serving lies to his third-worst category of deception. St. Thomas Aquinas labeled them mischievous and considered them mortal sins.

If some lies are automatically bad because they spring from bad or selfish motives, can other deceptions — those that the liar intends to accomplish good or to benefit other people — just as automatically be called good? Perhaps so. Think of the deceptions in which Dietrich Bonhoeffer engaged as he plotted to overthrow Hitler. Those lies were prompted by Bonhoeffer's desire to serve humanity and the truth that God recognizes. The destruction of a terrible evil, an end to the carnage of World War II and the restoration of freedom and democracy in Nazi-dominated Europe — those were Bonhoeffer's goals. Contrast them with Hitler's aims as he lied to the German people during and after his rise to the dictatorship. Hitler acted out of personal ambition and a lust for power. His lies were bad. Bonhoeffer's were good. The conclusion seems inescapable: bad motives make a bad lie; good motives make a good lie.

This equation — bad motive, bad lie; good motive, good lie — is a simple one and one human beings rely

on frequently to justify the deceptions they find it necessary or useful to practice. It is an equation that may
have passed through Lillian Carter's mind as she flat-
tered the reporter who was to question her so persis-
tently about her son's truthfulness, for example. Miss
Lillian's compliments seem like evidence of a conviction — shared by most of us — that putting someone
at her ease is the right thing to do even if it involves
fibbing. Most people would add that lies motivated by
the desire to spare another's feelings are justified under
a wide variety of circumstances. That was what Hugo
Grotius was suggesting when he wrote that it is ethical
to lie to anyone who needs or wants to be protected by
a deception. It is, in effect, how a mother reasons when
she misleads her child about the way a doctor's shot is
going to feel and how families rationalize deceiving a
dying man about his condition. Good motives make
good lies, people tell themselves. The equation is useful not only because it seems to justify deception but
because it paints so much of that deception white.

White lies and other lies meant to accomplish a good
end are not confined to family circles. Nor are they
heard only among friends and acquaintances. They fill
our lives and come to us from every imaginable source,
public and private, business and professional, near and
far. In this chapter, we will look at just a few of those
sources.

We have already seen how much the advertising industry owes to people's willingness to be lied to. It also owes a great deal to the advertisers' own willingness to lie. Not all ads are deceptive, naturally, but it is rare for one to be really truthful. The actual world bears little resemblance to the world shown by advertising. How many women do the laundry wearing designer outfits and with every hair in place? How many smile brightly as they scrub the bathroom? How many children run eagerly to the supper table and praise Mom lavishly for the food she offers? How many men rave about the fiber content of their breakfast cereal? Do antacids, cough medicines and decongestants really produce the instant relief they do on TV?

No. But advertising doesn't need to be an accurate reflection of the real world, most people would probably say. An ad is supposed to dramatize a single, simple idea: this product gets rid of headaches; that one cleans bathroom tiles. Advertising's job is to promote a product or a service, to introduce it to the public and get that public to buy or use it. Isn't that a legitimate goal? If a product doesn't sell, the company that makes it may go out of business. Money will be lost and so will jobs. Surely, preserving those jobs and saving that money are sufficient reason for a little exaggeration, perhaps even for outright misrepresentation. Where would detergent manufacturers be if admen and women didn't portray housework as fun? What would happen to tobacco farmers and cigarette makers if ads were honest about the dangers of smoking? What would become of the brewers of "lite" beers if professional athletes didn't appear on TV to tout their products? Do those big burly guys really drink "lite" beer? Does smoking cigarettes mean a sophisticated and successful lifestyle? What if it doesn't? Cigarettes and beer, and other products, too, need a market, people say, and providing that market justifies the deception.

Other types of lies are similarly excused as "white" in the name of business and a healthy economy. Some concern pollution. Everyone knows that pollution is a problem in the modern world. Toxic wastes spill from factories into rivers, lakes and streams. Foul-smelling gases pour from industrial smokestacks, poisoning the air and causing the acid rain that environmental scientists claim has already damaged the forests of the northeastern United States and much of Canada. Hazardous by-products of the manufacture of plastics and of chemical herbicides, pesticides and fertilizers are abandoned in illegal and inadequate dumps to seep into wells and public water supplies. Most dangerous of all, in the view of many, deadly nuclear radiation escapes from the nation's nuclear-fueled electric power plants. Radiation is a known cause of many diseases, cancer among them.

What is the solution to the pollution problem? The answer many give: force polluters to clean up after themselves. Pass new laws to compel industrialists to come up with safe ways of disposing of their wastes, to install more effective pollution-control devices and to end the practice of pouring pollutants — including nuclear pollutants — into the environment. Industry's response to that suggestion: it's too expensive. Business has to operate at a profit, its leaders point out, and if it has to pay for cleaning up its pollution, that profit will disappear. Plants and factories will shut down. Jobs will vanish. So will products like plastics, fertilizers and pesticides — products vital to the nation's economic well-being. If nuclear power plants close, too, the United States will become dangerously dependent on expensive and sometimes hard-to-get foreign oil.

Those are unthinkable possibilities. America needs its nuclear industry. Its factories must hum busily if we are to remain a rich and important international power. What better motive could there be for a few lies? And so people in business and industry do lie from time to time, denying their companies' illegal dumping; falsifying records to downplay the amount of pollution they cause; hiring scientists to produce reports that cast doubt on the idea of links between pollution and acid rain or between nuclear radiation and increased cancer rates and the like.

These fibs may give rise to others. Environmental activists, frustrated by what they see as industry's insistence on covering up a serious problem, may react by exaggerating the amount of pollution around the country. Or they may overstate the dangers posed by that pollution. In 1980, a Texas research firm conducted health tests on thirty-five former residents of the polluted Love Canal area of Niagara Falls, New York. According to its figures, eleven of those tested suffered from physical abnormalities that could be passed on to their children in the form of birth defects. Public concern, fanned by environmental groups, rose — until doctors from the federal Centers for Disease Control (CDC) in Atlanta, Georgia, revealed biases in the study's findings. According to the CDC, the Texas researchers had counted as birth defects such conditions as jaundice, cerebral palsy and pigeon toes, none of which is a true birth defect.

Environmentalists, businesspeople and advertisers are far from being the only ones who can claim good motives for lying. Take doctors and other health care professionals, for instance. They may be as likely to deceive a seriously ill patient as members of the patient's own family. It's easy to see why. The blunt truth about a catastrophic illness can be depressing, while a lie may be therapeutic. Deceiving patients gives them hope, and that hope may provide a psychological boost that will make their lives pleasanter. It even increases their chances of recovery, some doctors contend. Without the deception, sick people may despair, give up and prepare to die. Some will even commit suicide. What value has truth if it brings death?

Some doctors defend lies meant to protect patients in other ways. Those who work with victims of the disease AIDS (Acquired Immune Deficiency Syndrome), for example, may find their patients begging them to keep silent about their condition, or to deny to others that it exists. One case in which this happened involved the American entertainer Liberace. Liberace succumbed to AIDS in 1987; but his doctor concealed the nature of his illness from the public while he was alive, and when he died, cited heart disease as the cause.

Liberace's doctor must have felt he had reason enough to lie. AIDS is a terrifying condition, and many people fear both it and those who have contracted it. The disease invariably kills, and although virtually everyone who has studied it maintains that it cannot be spread through casual contact, some outside the medical community hesitate to take science's word for that. They believe they and their families run the risk of picking up AIDS from infected neighbors, co-workers, fellow students and others, and this belief has led to discrimination against AIDS patients. Many have been fired from jobs or made to move from rented houses or apartments. A few have had to leave towns where they have lived for years. Children with AIDS have been kept out of classes in a number of public schools. Even after death, the stigma of having been an AIDS victim may linger on, since the disease has so far largely affected homosexual men and drug addicts who pass the virus along by using infected intravenous needles. The extent of the discrimination against those with AIDS makes some doctors feel justified in lying to keep their patients' condition from becoming public knowledge.

Doctors and scientists who carry out research on new drugs and medical treatments also find themselves lying on the job. Typically, such research consists of giving the experimental therapy to one group of patients while treating a second, similar group with a harmless and ineffective look-alike, or placebo. If the first group shows an improvement and the second does not, that is an indication that the therapy works. In order for the research to show the most accurate results, though, neither group must know who is getting the placebo and who the real treatment. Knowing, scientists say, might lead the subjects to *believe* they were feeling better — or not feeling better — and that would affect the outcome of the experiment.

Isn't producing accurate scientific research a good reason to lie? Without placebo testing, many powerful healing drugs and preventive vaccines might never have reached the marketplace. What reasonable person would argue that lies that helped test the effectiveness of penicillin or a polio vaccine were immoral? Who would say that AIDS researchers would be wrong to lie in the interests of finding a cure for that disease?

Other types of scientific work may provide other motives for deception. Sir Isaac Newton, one of the most famous of all scientists, developed his ideas about gravity and the movements of the planets in the seventeenth century. At that time, scientific instruments were far cruder than they are today. Although those instruments proved to Newton's satisfaction that his theories were correct, they were not accurate enough to give him the extremely precise measurements he needed to make his results appear perfect to others. So Newton "fudged" his figures, refining and altering them until they matched his ideas in exact detail.

Modern-day scientists may falsify their research results, too. Researchers at leading American universities and at private research firms have been caught doing just that, reporting, for instance, greater progress in various areas of medical research than they have actually achieved. Their motive: to win funding for further research that will, they are convinced, deliver the results they have already claimed.

Of all the research frauds perpetrated in this century, perhaps the greatest was that of British psychologist Cyril Burt. Burt's field was the study of human intelligence, and it was his belief that intelligence is an inborn characteristic that cannot be changed as a child becomes older. He expounded on this theory in a number of scientific journals early in the century, and although not all psychologists accepted it (many believed that intelligence levels can be affected by such outside factors as health and upbringing), each article was greeted by enthusiastic and admiring letters. Some were followed up by supportive papers submitted by other scientists, as well. Burt's reputation grew with the years, and in 1946, he became the first psychologist in England to receive a knighthood. It was as Sir Cyril that he published his infamous "twin studies."

The twin studies seemed to prove conclusively that Burt's fixed-intelligence theory was correct. He and his research associates reported examining fifty-three pairs of identical twins who had been separated from each other at birth and raised in completely different types of households. Despite the disparities in their adoptive backgrounds and upbringings, each set of twins remained almost identical mentally. No environment was too harsh to dim the intelligence of a girl whose twin was bright. None was stimulating enough to raise that of a boy whose twin was dull.

Burt died in 1971, his public reputation as high as ever. Privately, though, psychologists were expressing doubts about his work. Years of study by other researchers around the world had demonstrated convincingly that intelligence levels are variable in individuals. And there were problems in Burt's studies of twins, it seemed. Vital details were missing. Descriptions of the intelligence tests administered to the twins were vague. And where were the men and women Burt had listed as research assistants? No one could find them. Where were the twins? No one could find them, either. By the mid-1970s, the truth was out: the studies were an utter fraud. Not only that, the earlier admiring letters and follow-up reports turned out to have been hoaxes as well. All had been composed by Burt himself under a variety of pseudonyms. His motive, like Newton's, was to convince the world of a theory he believed to be true.

Who else might find reason to lie in the interests of his or her work? Sheriff Frank Hackett did, and so have the hundreds of other local, state and federal law officers who have designed and carried out similar sting operations. Policemen and women use deceptive tactics in other situations, too, as we have seen. Some of them have been ingenious. In one instance, a quick-thinking officer kept a man from taking his own life by adjusting his collar and donning a black sweater so that he resembled a Roman Catholic priest. Believing that it was a man of God who was imploring him to go on living, the would-be suicide surrendered to rescuers. Law officers and special police agents have turned to deception to win freedom for people taken hostage, too, relying on tricks and lies to get kidnappers and terrorists to release their victims. Who would call them wrong?

The police are not the only liars in law-related fields. Many attorneys whose job it is to represent criminal defendants believe that they are justified in lying in court if that is what it takes to win their clients the not-guilty verdicts they seek. Other lawyers who stop short of lying themselves argue that it is ethical for them to permit their clients to testify to what they know to be untrue. After all, they say, under our system of law every defendant, even the guiltiest, is entitled to the best possible defense. How can a guilty person get that defense except through lies? "I don't see why we should not come out roundly and say that one of the functions of a lawyer is to lie for his client," one Boston attorney has said.

Other courtroom liars may include the expert witnesses who testify for the prosecution or the defense in criminal cases. A forensic scientist, convinced that a defendant is guilty even though the evidence is slight, might be tempted to overstate that evidence in order to ensure a conviction. A psychiatrist may lie about a convicted murderer's mental state in the hopes of keeping him from the electric chair — or sending him to it. Are such lies justified by the motives that prompt them? And what about those of us who are not doctors, lawyers or forensic experts? We, too, could find ourselves thinking we have good reason to lie in court. A woman who opposes capital punishment may be summoned as a potential juror in a murder case. If she lies, assuring the judge that she believes in the death penalty, she will be seated on the jury. (Anyone who admits to opposing capital punishment will be kept from jury duty in a capital case.) Once on the jury, she will have the chance to argue against an execution if the defendant is convicted.

Few people are much surprised to hear of lying in the courtroom or among members of the legal profession. Lawyers have traditionally been thought of as tricky or duplicitous. Most Americans, though, were surprised in the 1980s by repeated accounts of deceptions in the world of education. Some of the accounts had to do with college athletics; officials at a number of schools and colleges were found to have conspired to conceal the failing grades of their sports stars or to have paid those stars for their efforts on the field. Both practices are forbidden by the rules governing college athletics, but university coaches, teachers, administrators and trustees justified their deceptions with claims that they had acted in their schools' best interests. A winning team means happy alumni, they pointed out, and happy alumni contribute generously to their alma maters. That benefits all students, not just athletes.

Other cases of academic deception concerned testing. On the grade school level, it was revealed in 1987 that national achievement tests have been standardized so as to make it appear that many more students are above average than actually are. The inaccurate test results, of course, allow students, parents, teachers, school officials and the nation as a whole to feel better about their educational systems than they otherwise would. Also in 1987, Americans learned that colleges routinely fail to report the lowest Scholastic Aptitude Test (SAT) scores of their incoming freshmen. At the nation's most selective and prestigious private colleges, up to a quarter of the freshmen who are children of alumni, scholarship athletes and others may be left out of the SAT statistics. This practice, too, can benefit a school, administrators believe. By making it appear that a college's entrance standards are higher than they really are, they attract only the most outstanding applicants.

Many of the lies we see and hear in our daily lives come to us through the news media. Lies from politicians, lies from criminals, lies from financiers, lies from world leaders — the stories fill column after column and broadcast after broadcast. Some of the time, though, the lies come from reporters themselves. A few of these lies are the kind Thomas Aquinas called "jocose," tales invented to amuse or entertain. One example appeared in the now-defunct *New York Herald Tribune* throughout the fall of 1941. Week by week, readers of that paper followed the triumphs of the Plainfield Teachers College football team. Victories came regularly: Plainfield 12–Scott 0; Plainfield 24–Chesterton 0; Plainfield 27–Winona 3. The only trouble was, Plainfield was a fictional institution.

Another newspaper hoax took in hundreds of British readers in 1982. During the late winter of that year, people all over England had been bothered by poor television reception. Pictures wavered and static flashed across screens. At first, people were inclined to blame bad weather for the problem, but on April 1, a different explanation came to light. "Widespread television interference," began an article in the popular *Daily Mail*, "is being caused, not by unusual atmospheric conditions, but by 10,000 'rogue bras.' "

The story went on to give details. The bras had been made with supports of specially treated copper wire originally designed for fire alarm systems. The combination of body heat and friction from the wires rubbing against the bras' nylon material created static electricity. When the bras were worn by women technicians in the nation's television studios, this electricity caused interference. Among those who read the story was the chief engineer at the British Telecom broadcasting system, a man who had been assigned to locate the cause of the interference and put an end to it. The man telephoned his office and ordered a check on all British Telecom's women technicians. Imagine his chagrin when he realized it was April Fools' Day!

Other sources of newspaper fiction are to be found at the check-out counters of just about every supermarket and convenience store in the United States: weekly tabloids like the *National Enquirer* and the *Star*. "Sunbathing Man Bursts into Flames," screams one headline. "I Gave Birth to 17 Rabbits," cries another. Many of the tabloids' stories about sightings of unidentified flying objects, and all the articles about the U.S. government's efforts to cover them up, are based on forgeries of supposed presidential memos dating back to the 1950s.

Not all reportorial lies are so titillating or amusing. Not all are aimed at the public, either. Sometimes reporters feel they must turn to falsehood in the interests of getting an important story. Two who did were Bob Woodward and Carl Bernstein of the *Washington Post.* Woodward and Bernstein were among those who took the lead in exposing the Nixon administration's Watergate lies.

In the process, they relied on a few fibs of their own. Once, one of them telephoned a member of the White House staff, identified himself as a friend and led the staffer into a frank discussion of Watergate. At other times, Woodward and Bernstein convinced White House aides — falsely — that others had said damaging things about their part in the cover-up. Alarmed, the aides would quickly offer their own version of events. After Nixon's resignation, the reporters described their deceptive methods in *All the President's Men,* a book they wrote together. Neither felt the need to justify or explain the lies, and Americans did not ask them to. No justification was required, most believed. The reporters' motives had been good. Good motives, good lies.

Really? Sissela Bok, the Harvard ethicist, has some reservations. While acknowledging that the *Post*'s Watergate reporting served the country well, and conceding that the deceptions may indeed have been essential to that reporting, Bok questions the total absence of any suggestion that a moral issue might have been at stake. "No one seems to have stopped to think that there was a problem in using deceptive means," she writes. "No one weighed the reasons for and against doing so. There was no reported effort to search for honest alternatives, or to distinguish among different forms and degrees of deception, or to consider whether some circumstances warranted it more than others." And there should have been, she concludes.

Why? Isn't the "good motive, good lie" equation enough to justify deceptions like Woodward and Bernstein's? Doesn't it also justify other well-meant deceptions like those we have examined in this chapter?

Many ethicists think not. There are several reasons why. One revolves around the difficulty of determining what a liar's motive really is.

Did Woodward and Bernstein lie to the targets of their investigation solely out of a passion for truth? Or did they think, as well, about the fame and fortune that would — and did — await those who uncovered the secrets of Watergate? If the motive for their lies was the latter, even in part, would we see those lies in a different light? Judge them more harshly?

What about the industrialists who seek to deceive lawmakers and the public about pollution? Do they think exclusively of others' jobs and the national interest and never of corporate or personal gain? What about the researchers who came up with the misleading findings about the health of the Love Canal refugees? Did it ever cross their mind that if their results fit in with environmental biases, they might win new research contracts? What about people in advertising? It seems obvious that a desire for personal profit operates with them, just as it must for scientific researchers who exaggerate their successes in the search for funding.

It seems obvious — but is it? How can any of us know what a liar's motives truly are? A researcher may be truly convinced that more money, and more research, will produce a medical breakthrough. It is possible that there are those in business and advertising who are motivated purely by altruism — the desire to benefit others. And who can know for sure what Timothy Cooney's motives were when he forged a covering letter for his manuscript? People assumed he acted selfishly, but he could argue that he thought he was giving his editor exactly what he wanted. After all, editors and publishers do promote books by soliciting recommendations and admiring "blurbs" from well-known men and women. Sometimes they pay those men and women for their trouble in looking over a manuscript. Couldn't Cooney have convinced himself that he was saving his editor the bother of going through all that? That would make his motive altruistic, too.

Who can even say what reasons President Nixon and his aides and advisors may have had as they began lying about Watergate? Perhaps they genuinely felt that keeping the administration in power was a patriotic duty essential to the country's well-being. Nixon could boast of some remarkable accomplishments during his first term of office. In February 1972, he traveled to the People's Republic of China on a "journey for peace." He was the first U.S. president to go to the People's Republic — communist China — and his visit did much to open up that country to the West and to Western ideas. Three months later, Nixon signed a major nuclear weapons treaty with the Soviet Union, another step toward easing world tensions. Could Nixon have honestly thought that his Watergate deceptions would be justified by further such accomplishments in his second term?

It works the other way, too, of course. Just as we cannot be certain that a liar's motives are bad, we cannot know that they are good. Think about social white lies, for example, and the motives behind them. White liars assure themselves and others that their motives are of the best, to put people at ease, to bridge a social awkwardness or to make someone happy. But are all social white lies uttered for such purposes? Are those who tell them always as concerned with others' feelings as they are with their own? Take the mother who lies to her child about how a doctor's shot will feel. She says she is acting to protect him. Couldn't there be a bit of "I'll-do-anything-at-all-to-get-this-kid-to-stop-crying" mixed in?

Couldn't there be a little laziness mixed in also? It takes an effort to explain to a three-year-old that the doctor's shot will hurt, but only for a little while, that it is necessary because it will make him well, or keep him from getting sick, and so on and on. It seems easier just to fib. Perhaps it seemed easier to Bob Woodward and Carl Bernstein, too. Remember that Sissela Bok criticized them for their failure to make an "effort" to search for honest ways of getting the Watergate information they needed.

In some cases of lying by reporters, laziness has been much more in evidence. When civil unrest and rioting broke out in Northern Ireland in the late 1960s and early 1970s, one *New York Daily News* journalist gained wide attention with his dramatic stories from that nation. The reports he filed brought the horror of Northern Ireland's political and religious strife home to American readers in vivid terms. Those reports described bloody clashes between Catholics and Protestants and made clear the plight of the individuals — especially the children — caught in the middle. Moving as they were, however, the stories were not true. The reporter had made up people and pretended to interview them and invented incidents that never happened. That was easier, apparently, than going out and getting the real story. In much the same way, a woman who worked for the *Washington Post* wrote a Pulitzer Prize–winning series of articles about heroin use in the city. Among the addicts she claimed to have talked to was an eight-year-old named Jimmy. Jimmy did not exist. The reporter had concocted him for the purpose of highlighting Washington's youthful addict problem — which *did* exist — and of pushing city and federal authorities into doing something about it. Good motive. Good lie?

Other "well-intentioned" lies might never be told if liars were willing to make the effort to get their points across without relying on deception or to accomplish their goals by honest means. Law enforcement officers have options other than sting operations by which they can solve crimes and hunt down criminals, for example. As we saw, lack of effort was one charge leveled against Sheriff Frank Hackett in the wake of his television sting. Laziness seems to have been a factor in the case of the English authorities who suppressed predictions about traffic deaths if a seat belt rule became law. Why couldn't they have published the report — and used it as a basis for creating an educational campaign aimed at making drivers more aware of their responsibilities toward others? Truth would have been served and so would the cause of highway safety.

Great harm can be done when people assume that good motives are enough to outweigh the possibility of bad consequences and that lies must be tolerated simply because they are intended to have a good effect. U.S. presidents and other civilian and military leaders made such an assumption as they lied to the American people about Vietnam in the fifties, sixties and seventies. Those lies grew out of what the leaders saw as the best of motives: the determination to keep the nations of Southeast Asia from falling to communist-led dictatorships. Such dictatorships are not pleasant for most of those who live under them. Their citizens lack the freedoms Americans take for granted — freedom of speech, the press and religion, for example, and the right to move about at will. Most also lack the material possessions we take for granted — automobiles, private houses and the like. Surely, American leaders assured themselves, keeping communism out of Southeast Asia, and trying to bring democracy and prosperity to its peoples, was a cause good enough to justify almost any lie. After all, they may have argued, Bonhoeffer's cause seemed to excuse his lies, and the World War II Allied cause to have justified the hoax of the man who never was. And so the decision makers of the Vietnam War neglected to look beyond their motives for lying and spared no thought for the consequences if those lies were found out.

Cyril Burt also failed to consider the consequences

of his lies, and assumed the right to resort to fraud in the interests of a theory in which he believed. Perhaps he reasoned that the great Sir Isaac Newton had done something similar. If so, he forgot that Newton's deceptions did no more than make a good proof perfect. Burt went much further, fabricating his "studies" from start to finish.

The effects of his fabrications were far-reaching. British educators, accepting them as scientific fact, ordered all children in state-run schools to undergo testing shortly after their eleventh birthday. Those who did well were sent to good schools and, later, to universities. Those who did not do well — the vast majority — were shunted off to less rigorous institutions or began training for jobs. For them, all chances for higher education and professional work were gone. Although this testing system is no longer in place in England, it governed the personal destinies of most members of an entire society for more than a decade.

In the United States, as well, education has been adversely affected by the deceptions put forward in its name. Lying about the academic accomplishments of college athletes is clearly unfair to all those students who work hard for their A's and B's — or even C's and D's. Pretending that elementary school students are learning more than they are weakens a school system by making the public complacent about it and leading that public to assume — incorrectly — that it needs no improving or reforming. Lying to high school juniors and seniors about how well they must score on their SATs to get into a good college could keep many of them from even applying to schools for which they are perfectly well qualified. What an interference with their liberty of judgment that is!

A doctor may assume he or she has a right to lie to protect a patient with a disease like AIDS. But what if the lie results in an AIDS victim's marrying or donating blood to a blood bank? Either could cause the disease to spread. Doctors who test new drugs argue that obedience to the scientific method requires some deception. Some may further believe that as knowledgeable professionals they are entitled to deceive lay people — much as adults may assume that they have a right to lie to children. Perhaps doctors should rethink both positions. Sissela Bok tells of research carried out on two groups of Mexican-American women in a southwestern state. The study's aim was to test the effectiveness of a new type of birth control pill. Researchers told the women in each group that they would be getting genuine birth control. In one case, that was the truth; in the other, a lie. It is not difficult to guess one outcome of that experiment. The lie affected not only the women but also their children, children who must have been unwanted, since their mothers had been seeking birth control. The researchers felt justified. But were they?

The telling of a lie — even in a good cause — can

harm the innocent. It can do damage to the cause itself, too, as many a well-intentioned liar has discovered. Americans lost the will to fight in Vietnam as they learned how they had been misled about conditions there. Interest in missing children flagged as people found out how others had exaggerated the problem. Much of the public has come to regard industrial polluters and doom-crying environmentalists with the same degree of skepticism. Many ignore the words and warnings of both. People take advertising with a large grain of salt and doubt the truthfulness of a great deal of what they read and hear in the news media. It seems as if Immanuel Kant had a point, after all. Lies, including lies told for the best of reasons, do appear to constitute "a wrong done to mankind generally." They create doubt and suspicion where none existed. They undermine the confidence that people must have in one another if society is to flourish. They are indeed the "plague" of which St. Augustine warned.

Or so some people would say. But take a deception of the kind put forth by New York City's Coalition for the Homeless, a group that works on behalf of the needy. That deception — if it can be called a deception — involved a nine-year-old boy named David Bright. In 1986, David was living with his mother and her three other children in a run-down Manhattan "welfare hotel." The five shared two bedrooms and a bath and had nowhere to cook or prepare meals. Each got less than

$6 a day for food, transportation and personal expenses. Often, they had nothing to eat.

Thanks to members of the coalition, David got the chance to tell his story to a committee of the U.S. Congress. The coalition paid the boy's way to Washington, D.C., where he testified before a group of representatives. "It hurts to be hungry," David said.

It does, and David frequently went hungry. But why? Because government neglects the poor, as the coalition was charging? Or because David's bus occasionally arrived at school too late for him to receive the free meal he was entitled to there, as New York City officials claimed after reading about his testimony?

Questioned later by reporters, David agreed that his bus had been late a couple of times the previous week. Breakfast was over by the time he reached his classroom. That was why he had gone hungry on those days. The coalition had lied to Congress, New York's mayor said angrily, and used David for its own dishonest purposes.

The mayor had a point — but so did the coalition. David may have missed one or two meals because of a late bus, but it was also true that his mother had no cooking facilities and only $6 a day with which to feed her son and provide for his other needs. In a city where a bus ride costs $1 and a plain hamburger $2.50, that's just not enough. Wasn't it the real truth that David was hungry because his family was not getting all the help

it needed? Wasn't that the truth that God would recognize?

Dietrich Bonhoeffer might well have said so, arguing that just as it would be "correct" for a child to lie
about his father's alcoholism in order to protect the
higher truth of his family's unity, it would be right to
bend the truth in the interests of getting Congress to
understand the truth about hunger in America. But some
see a problem with this argument. What, they ask, if a
child chooses to protect his family by falsely denying
that his father is abusing a younger child, or commit-
ting incest with her? Not only would such a lie shield
the abuser; it would permit the abuse to continue. Would
Bonhoeffer call that lie correct? That is one big problem with the "good motive, good lie" equation. Which
causes are good *enough* to merit lies for their sake?

Which causes are good at all? What does "good"
mean? Who defines it in a particular case? Who de-
cides that one motive is good and another bad?

Dietrich Bonhoeffer was positive that the mission to
overthrow Hitler was sufficient motive to justify lying,
and most of us would say the same. Not everyone,
though. There are those in the world, even in the United
States, who share Hitler's ideas. Hitler was right, these
people would say, in his belief that white northern Eu-
ropeans are racially superior. He was right to persecute
Jews and others. He was right to suppress his domestic
enemies and right to go to war against his foreign ones.

The neo- (new) Nazis who think this way would not see Bonhoeffer's motives — or his lies — as good. To them, Hitler was the one with virtue on his side.

It is not difficult to refute a point of view as extreme as this one. Hitler is regarded by most as history's cruelest and most brutal dictator — and possibly as its most insane, as well. If ever people deserved to be plotted against and lied to, those people were Germany's Nazi leaders. If ever a person could be said to have taken a moral stand and to have lied justly for the sake of a higher truth, that person was Bonhoeffer. Between him and Hitler, the ethical distinctions were sharp and the moral judgments clear-cut. It is not always that way, however. Most of the moral dilemmas people face are more ambiguous.

One such dilemma confronting Americans today centers around the issue of abortion. A 1973 ruling by the U.S. Supreme Court confirmed a woman's right to choose to seek an abortion during the early months of pregnancy. As soon as that "pro-choice" decision was announced, a "right-to-life" movement sprang up across the country. The movement was organized by men and women who believe that the aborting of an unborn child amounts to the murder of a human being. Their goal: to put an end to legal abortion, either through new court decisions or by passing local, state and federal measures against the practice.

The anti-abortionists' goal has been endorsed by Ro-

man Catholic church leaders and by some Protestant
and Jewish groups. Right-to-lifers believe wholeheart-
edly in the moral rightness of their cause and they pursue it vigorously. Even one abortion prevented is a gain,
they feel, and in some instances, they have sought to
win that gain by deceptive means.

One of the anti-abortionists' misleading tactics has
been to place newspaper and magazine ads that appear
to be for pregnancy counseling or birth control centers.
The ads attract girls and women who are looking for
calm, objective advice about how to handle an unwanted pregnancy. That is not what a woman hears
when she visits such a clinic, however. Instead, she
gets a lecture from dedicated anti-abortionists determined to convince her that if she ends the pregnancy,
she will have murdered someone. She may also be
shown pictures of aborted fetuses or find herself sitting
through the screening of a movie like *The Silent Scream.*

This film is a powerful piece of anti-abortion propaganda. Its most dramatic sequence shows a twelve-
week-old fetus that is apparently being aborted. At one
point, the fetus appears to flinch violently and open its
mouth in a soundless howl of agony.

According to a panel of experts consisting of five
members of the American College of Obstetricians and
Gynecologists, however, the fetus could neither have
flinched nor screamed. Fetuses aborted in the twelfth
week have nervous systems far too undeveloped to al-

low them to feel pain, the doctors asserted. One panel member explained how the deceptive sequence was shot. "Right before [the film's narrator] says the fetus is reacting and fighting aggressively, he has the film in very slow motion. Then as the [abortion] begins, he turns it on to regular speed. It's really very misleading."

But it is misleading in a good cause. Right-to-lifers believe that abortion is murder. Doesn't that belief make their deceptions moral? If you saw someone about to commit what you considered to be murder, wouldn't you do anything in your power to stop him or her — even lie?

Would you? Would Immanuel Kant? It is hard to say for sure. Kant wrote that lying is wrong, even under the most drastic of circumstances. In a real-life situation, though, would anyone live up to such a philosophy? Remember St. Augustine's lament, as he faced the dilemma of whether or not to lie to protect someone: "Often . . . human sympathy overcomes me." Wouldn't it overcome Kant as well?

What would St. Augustine have to say about lies in the anti-abortion cause? Bear in mind that many anti-abortionists act out of religious conviction. The Roman Catholic church forbids abortion, and has since 1869, unless it is necessary to save the mother's life. If a Catholic lies to a woman with the intention of getting her to change her mind about having the operation, has he or she lied "in the teaching of religion"? Such a lie would fall into Augustine's first — deadliest — category. It would be the type of lie he said must be avoided "under any circumstances."

How would St. Thomas Aquinas regard lies meant to prevent abortion? He believed that the sin of lying is lessened if the lie is in a good cause. Yet, like Augustine, he lived long before the church condemned the deliberate termination of a pregnancy.

What would the Protestant reformer Martin Luther have felt about a person lying out of religious motives to prevent an abortion? Unlike Augustine, Luther stoutly defended lies meant to serve truth and the faith.

Would someone like Dietrich Bonhoeffer defend a lie to stop an abortion? If abortion really is murder, then that is the truth that God knows, the higher truth that Bonhoeffer believed to be more important than literal human veracity. Speeding up a film sequence, or slowing it down, seems a trivial bit of misdirection compared to the truth that underlies the right-to-life movement. The anti-abortionists' motives justify their deceptions.

Really? Doesn't the way a person feels about that statement depend on how he or she feels about abortion itself? Anyone who believes that a woman has the moral right to make her own decisions about her own health and her own body, and to decide for herself whether or not to end a pregnancy, will see the pro-choice position as the ethical one. He or she will feel justified in lying if necessary to defend the higher truth of that position. And that liar might be the one to win the support of such a man as the Protestant minister Bonhoeffer. Many Protestant and Jewish leaders are pro-choice. (So are some Catholics, including, despite the church's official position, a few members of the Catholic clergy.) For those who believe in a woman's right to abortion, it is the pro-choicers who seem to have the good on their side.

Sorting out the good and the bad is difficult in other moral, social and political situations as well. Which is the better cause — supplying jobs and boosting the economy or preventing pollution? Tracking down the guilty or protecting the innocent? Promoting a product or safeguarding public health? Avoiding discrimination against the victims of AIDS or stopping the spread of an epidemic? Telling an apocryphal tale to alert Americans to welfare cheating or dressing up a boy's story to inform the nation that its children are going hungry?

There is a final problem with the "good motive, good lie" equation. It is this: the men and women who believe most deeply in a cause, and who most strongly defend lies told for its sake, are the very ones who run the greatest risk of losing the ability to think clearly and critically about the ethical implications of those lies. Absorbed by the merits of their motive, they overlook the right of others to what Hugo Grotius called liberty of judgment. What these people see as their "right" to lie blinds them to others' right to the truth. In the end, they may fall into the trap of regarding the deceptions they practice as being just as necessary, just as important and valuable, as the cause itself.

Bob Woodward and Carl Bernstein appear to have fallen into a small trap of this kind as they lied to extract the truth about Watergate from the Nixon White House. As Bok points out, the two never mentioned any doubt as to the correctness of their investigative techniques.

The trap in which U.S. political and military leaders found themselves as a result of their Vietnam War deceptions was larger and more deadly. From the outset, those leaders failed to question their motives — or their lies. The truth about Vietnam, about how its people felt and what they wanted, had less significance to many in Washington, D.C., than did their own conviction that a new communist government must not be permitted to come to power in Southeast Asia. Propaganda was constructed and lies told to support that conviction. Before long, the propaganda and the lies came to seem more real to the liars than did the truth about world politics.

People in advertising who promote tobacco, diet pills, hair restorers and other useless or harmful products seem not to question their determination to profit at the expense of others. They, too, have fallen into a trap, a trap that allows them to practice deception in the name of business and the national economy. Environmental activists, scientists, doctors, lawyers and others who justify lying as a necessary part of their working lives similarly appear to feel that their personal and professional interests place them somehow above the need to respect others' right to the truth. And we ourselves show that we feel the same way, and have fallen into large or small traps of our own, as we find more and more reasons — and better and better ones — to lie in public and in private, to strangers and to loved ones, even to ourselves. The result, in the words of *Time* magazine's 1987 cover story on ethics, is that America has become a nation "assaulted by sleaze, scandals and hypocrisy."

Can something be done to clear up the sleaze? To end the scandals and hypocrisy and get Americans to tighten up their moral standards? Can we become a more ethical nation?

6
Laws, Regulations and Ethics

An ethical America. An America in which everyone, public officials and private citizens alike, displays a regard for truth. A nation of people who understand that lies and deceptions, however trivial or harmless seeming, however well meant or even necessary, carry a potential for inflicting great damage. A moral America. That is the goal. How do we achieve it?

"When most people talk about morals, they are concerned with laws and regulations and codes," says Daniel Callahan. Callahan is director of the Institute of Society, Ethics and the Life Sciences, at Hastings-on-Hudson, New York. He co-founded the institute, usually referred to as the Hastings Center, in 1969.

Callahan knew what he was talking about. To many people, law enforcement does seem to be the best, maybe the only, way to keep people honest. And so they prod legislators into writing laws and passing them, and encourage the police and other law enforcement agencies to put the laws into action. The United States has laws against stealing and cheating. It has laws against dumping toxic wastes and against lying about it, against fraud and embezzlement, against forgery, bribery, counterfeiting and all the rest. Anyone who breaks one of these laws stands the chance of being fined or sent to prison.

Nor is it only private citizens whose honesty and truthfulness our society tries to ensure through rules and regulations. Many local, state and federal laws are aimed at keeping government honest. The federal Freedom of Information Act, for instance, entitles Americans to ask to see any record maintained by an agency of the executive (presidential) branch of the federal government. Once the request has been made in proper form, the agency must make the information available. Only if that information falls into a category that is considered exempt — national security, for example — may the request be refused. News reporters and others used the Freedom of Information Act extensively to help them uncover the truth about Watergate and the Vietnam War.

Another federal law aimed at promoting public honesty is the Ethics in Government Act. This act, passed by Congress in 1978, grew directly out of the Watergate scandal. One of its sections provides for special court-appointed prosecutors to look into charges of illegal or unethical behavior by government officials. That

provision makes it impossible for the officials to protect themselves by claiming that their own internal in-
vestigations have shown no wrongdoing.

Other agencies of government operate with an eye
to honesty in the private sector. The federal Food and
Drug Administration (FDA) has been responsible, since
1906, for checking that the foods, medicines and cos-
metics advertised and sold in this country are safe and
that they live up to the claims made for them. In 1987,
the FDA took action against nine companies that manufacture skin care lotions, charging them with falsely
asserting that their products "prevent, postpone and
minimize the effects of the aging process" and "re-
create the structure of a young skin." No product can
do that, the FDA stated. Later that same year, the FDA
levied a $2 million fine against Beech-Nut, the baby
food company, as a penalty for advertising as "apple
juice" a concoction of beet sugar, cane sugar syrup
and other such ingredients.

The Federal Trade Commission (FTC), established
in 1915, also plays a role in monitoring commercial
advertising. Among other things, the agency has taken
a stand against dishonest celebrity endorsements. Two
1978 targets were singer Pat Boone and his daughter
Debbie. The Boones were paid to appear in a television
ad for a skin cream called Acne-Statin, which they
promoted as having been a "real help" in keeping
Debbie's skin free of blemishes. This could not be true,

the FTC contended, since there was no scientific evidence whatsoever that Acne-Statin did anything to help the complexion. The Boones were ordered to withdraw their endorsement and to help pay for refunds to dissatisfied Acne-Statin buyers.

Other agencies function in other areas. The Environmental Protection Agency (EPA) was set up by Congress in 1970 as Americans became increasingly aware of the health threats posed by the careless releasing and outright dumping of poisonous materials. The EPA is charged with seeing to it that toxic wastes and other hazardous materials are managed safely. It is also supposed to make sure that business and industry report accurately and honestly about the amount of pollution they produce and its level of toxicity.

Poisonous materials are likewise one concern of the Nuclear Regulatory Commission (NRC), set up in 1974 to assume some of the duties of the former Atomic Energy Commission. In the case of the NRC, the materials to be regulated are specifically radioactive. The agency also watches over nuclear power plant safety, the production of nuclear fuels and so on. Like other federal, state and local regulators, NRC commissioners and staff members frequently find themselves dealing with the dishonest. It is not uncommon for nuclear plant owners and operators to try to cover up evidence of faulty plant design and construction and of plant safety hazards — even of accidents and near accidents. In

1987, the NRC denied an operating permit to a new nuclear plant in Seabrook, New Hampshire, on the grounds that its owners had only pretended to have worked out a plan for protecting nearby residents in the case of an accident.

Government is not alone in relying on rules and regulations in an attempt to keep people honest. Nongovernment organizations — many of them so-called public interest groups — are also part of the effort.

The United States has hundreds, if not thousands, of such groups. Some, like Common Cause, Freedom Foundation, the Committee for Congressional Responsibility and the American Civil Liberties Union, devote themselves particularly to monitoring the ethics of men and women in government. Others are less concerned with political honesty than with honesty in the marketplace. Consumers Union conducts tests on consumer products and issues regular reports on their safety, dependability and cost. The Union of Concerned Scientists has a special interest in the nuclear power industry and in pushing for its stricter regulation and for greater openness and truthfulness among those who own and run the nation's nuclear plants. Groups like the Sierra Club, the National Wildlife Federation and the Environmental Defense Fund pursue honesty with regard to pollution and the environment.

How well does public and private regulation work? In the vast majority of cases, well enough. No industrialist wants to have to pay a fine because he or she has concealed the extent of a company's pollution, and lied about it. No politician wants his or her unethical behavior investigated by a special prosecutor. Private citizens do not want the force of the law brought to bear against them because of some dishonest act of theirs.

But no one would try to claim that regulation alone is enough to get people to act morally and ethically. One reason is that regulatory agencies, and the rules themselves, are subject to political pressure and private manipulation. In 1987, for instance, a number of people in Congress and around the country were calling for the resignation of Nuclear Regulatory Commissioner Thomas M. Roberts. Four years earlier, Roberts had supplied a Louisiana power company with secret NRC documents relating to safety violations in a plant it owned. In 1986, Victor Stello, Jr., executive director of the NRC, coached an official at another nuclear power company, telling him "not to give a definite response" to NRC questions about unsafe conditions in one of the facilities for which he was responsible.

Manipulation and pressure can come from higher up on the political ladder. From the time he took office as president in 1981, Ronald Reagan maintained that honoring requests for records under the Freedom of Information Act threatened national security. In 1986, he succeeded in getting Congress to weaken the law by broadening the categories that are exempt from such requests. The Reagan administration sought to overturn the special prosecutor provision of the 1978 Ethics in Government Act, too. And many Americans complained that agencies like the EPA, FDA and FTC were lax in their rule making and enforcement during the Reagan years. Administration officials disagreed. Too much government regulation doesn't ensure honesty, they said. It merely hurts business and makes it harder for people to earn a profit.

Another reason that regulations and enforcement have not succeeded in eliminating the "sleaze" in American life has to do with the way they approach the problem of deception and dishonesty. Both assume a legalistic and mechanical point of view. Both are aimed at detecting, preventing, uncovering and punishing specific deceitful acts. Both attempt to impose morality upon people from the outside. And that cannot really be done.

Acting morally or ethically is not the same as acting legally. Ethics, says Rushworth M. Kidder, a columnist for the *Christian Science Monitor,* is "obedience to the unenforceable." Lester C. Thurow, dean of the Sloan School of Management at the Massachusetts Institute of Technology, agrees. "Ethics does not consist of asking one's lawyer, 'Is it legal?' " Thurow says. "The question, 'Is it right?' is not the same as 'Is it legal?' Yet most Americans act as if it were so." What is needed, he believes, is a way to help them under-

stand the difference between "legal" and "ethical" —
and the importance of the latter.

What might that way be? A possibility some suggest: require men and women in business and the
professions to abide by strict ethical codes. The codes
would be written in such a way as to force doctors,
lawyers, executives and others to think about the moral
implications of their actions and decisions before they
commit themselves to either.

Will codes work? Many Americans doubt it. "Every
employee here . . . signs our code of ethics," said a
spokesperson for one New York City financial consult-
ing firm in 1987. It's the same for those working in
other financial houses. Yet one scandal after another
rocked the American business world in the mid-1980s.
The codes did nothing to stop that. Scandals struck in
other professions, too, despite the ethical standards that
were supposed to govern them. Men and women sign
the codes or agree to observe the standards, then ignore
both in their daily lives and as they go about their work.
Even when the codes have the force of law, they may
not be enough to keep people honest. The legal profession is generally regarded as harboring a considerable
percentage of the dishonest or sleazy, despite a 1986
Supreme Court ruling that requires attorneys to reveal
any client's attempt to lie under oath.

The reason for the codes' failure is simple, ethicists
say. In today's competitive world, individuals regard

themselves and their own interests as more important than society and its interests. They do not seem to understand the importance of the community as a whole, and forget that what affects one person affects us all. Can they be taught to distinguish between illegal and unethical, and made to see that the latter can be as damaging and destructive as the former? They can, many say, if they receive such instruction before embarking on their working lives — in graduate school, perhaps.

It was with this thought in mind that U.S. businessman John Shad made a $20 million donation to the Harvard Business School in the spring of 1987. The money was intended to cover a portion of the cost of setting up a $30 million ethics program there.

Shad's gift came because of his conviction that learning how to think and act ethically is a must for every business school student. That does not necessarily mean requiring all students to attend special classes devoted to memorizing rules of ethics. Rather, it means using every course they take to get across to them the idea that business must be conducted along ethical lines. If this is done and students grow to understand that making moral and socially aware business decisions is as important as making a profit, the business world will become a more honest and ethical place, Shad and others believe.

Other professions could also become more honest as a study of ethics is introduced into the nation's grad schools. Among the few courses the Harvard Law School requires all students to attend is one in legal ethics. Ethics classes are considered especially important for law students, since so many attorneys end up in politics and government. Many of those implicated in the Watergate scandal were lawyers. Nixon himself was one. The Harvard Law School course was added to the curriculum in the wake of that scandal. Besides offering instruction in ethics, law schools may require students to pass a special ethics examination during their final year of study. Some medical schools are beginning to place more emphasis on teaching personal and professional ethics, as well.

In some places, courses in professional ethics are also found at the undergraduate level. The engineering department at the Georgia Institute of Technology encourages students to attend an elective in which they examine the moral implications of events like the disastrous U.S. space shuttle flight of January 28, 1986. Just over a minute into that flight, a poorly designed rocket seal gave way. Flames spurted from the rocket, rupturing the shuttle's main fuel tank and igniting its half-million-gallon load of highly explosive liquid oxygen and hydrogen. The spacecraft blew to bits, killing all seven astronauts aboard.

It was a tragedy that need not have happened, a Georgia Tech professor reminds students. On the night of January 27, engineers at the company that had manufactured the defective seal warned their bosses that just such an accident was possible and begged them to ask officials at the National Aeronautics and Space Administration (NASA) to delay the launch. The bosses, knowing how eager NASA was to move ahead quickly with the shuttle program, decided to pretend they had never heard the warning. Together, professor and students discuss that decision — and the ethical and community-conscious considerations that should have gone into its making.

Are college- and graduate-level ethics courses enough to make Americans aware of their moral responsibilities toward their fellow citizens? They can help, certainly. But few people believe that they can do the whole job. In the first place, they say, the efforts of universities to offer such courses are all too often only halfhearted. Many schools appear to be more interested in seeming to promote ethical thinking than in actually doing it. Until receiving John Shad's $20 million, the critics point out, administrators at the Harvard Business School displayed a remarkable lack of concern for teaching ethics, repeatedly ignoring calls from outside the school for mandatory courses in the subject. Nor have Harvard officials ever offered a tenured (permanent) position to anyone qualified to teach business ethics.

In addition to the lack of administrative interest, many see a lack of student interest. Enrollment in Harvard

Business School's sole ethics-only course, Ethical Aspects of Corporate Policy, dropped from 155 in 1986 to 57 a year later. That was out of a total student body of sixteen hundred. At the same time, over four hundred students were finding room in their schedules for a course called Power and Influence. This bluntly named offering was being taught by a man who lacked any training whatsoever in ethics.

A third disadvantage of relying on universities to fill the need for instruction in ethics is that relatively few people are going to get it there. Most Americans stop their education short of the graduate level; a degree from a two- or four-year college, a high school diploma or a grade school certificate — that's all for millions of men and women. Where are those people to receive ethical training? They must get it somewhere: ethics needs to be a part of what goes on in shipyards and on construction sites as well as in lawyers' offices and corporate board rooms.

Some say the answer lies with the nation's public school systems. High school students could discuss public ethics in U.S. history classes, they suggest, or in government or problems of democracy courses. Ethical debates can arise in science classrooms, too, as teachers bring up the moral dilemmas encountered by researchers who may be tempted to make their results look a little — or a lot — better than they truly are. Literature courses can serve as places for discussions of ethics as students talk over the words and actions of the characters in novels, plays and short stories. Even students of junior high age ought to be learning community values and moral responsibility, many believe.

Others contend that letting ethical instruction wait until junior high is waiting too long. "I . . . [do not] believe that ethics can be taught past the age of ten," Felix G. Rohatyn, a senior partner in a New York financial firm, told graduating students at Long Island University in 1987. In Rohatyn's view, a person's ethical education needs to begin at least as early as grade school.

Some U.S. elementary schools are already making an effort to introduce students to the subject. A public interest group based in Texas, the American Institute for Character Education, has designed a curriculum to get young students talking about concepts like citizenship and social obligations. That program is in use in over thirty thousand classrooms in forty-five states. A second such curriculum has been produced at the Quest National Center in Columbus, Ohio.

Elementary school teachers may use their own initiative to get children thinking about ethical matters. Like everyone else, grade-schoolers face moral dilemmas every day of their lives. They see pupils cheating in class. Someone's lunch money disappears and someone else thinks — but only thinks — he knows who is responsible. Teachers may take advantage of such situations to get the ethical debate going. Should a person tell on the cheater? Name the suspected thief? Or should people just keep silent and mind their own business? As the discussion progresses, teachers may try to elicit certain reactions from students. They may even drop hints about their own moral standards and ideals. That's an excellent way to begin teaching ethics.

It can also be an excellent way for a teacher to get into trouble. Not everyone agrees with the idea that ethics should be part of the public school curriculum. Many oppose it fiercely, especially in grade school.

The teaching of ethics and morality should be a private family affair, say those who are against schools' getting involved in this area. Children should not be forming their moral and ethical standards on the basis of ideas handed out by whatever stranger happens to be their second or third-grade teacher, or their high school biology or history teacher, either. Nor should students be asked to learn from curricula that come from who-knows-what public interest group. It is up to parents to teach morals and to pass their own values along to their own children. If parents want to, they may seek help in this from rabbis, priests, ministers or others in positions of moral authority. But not from public school teachers or textbooks.

Critics of the public school teaching of ethics have some good points on their side. No mother wants her child influenced by ideas that seriously conflict with what she is trying to teach at home. No father wants to hear from his child that a teacher's standards are right and his are wrong. Parents may also worry that a specific learning program will be more concerned with pushing a particular social or political point of view than with promoting ethics generally. What many critics fear most, though, is that in the country's public schools, the teaching of ethics will become mixed up with the teaching of religion.

It could happen. Many people confuse ethics and religion. Actually, they are quite different.

Ethics is, of course, an essential part of religion. As we saw in chapter 3, all the world's leading religions are founded on an idea of the universal truth and goodness of a Supreme Being. Each encourages its faithful to reflect that truth and goodness by living and acting morally.

But religions are founded on more than a consideration of ethics. They are also based on dogma, formally stated doctrines that are proclaimed by the leaders of each religion.

Dogma differs from religion to religion. According to Christian dogma, Jesus, the Messiah, was crucified and rose from the dead. Jewish people reject that idea. For them, the Messiah is still to come. Muslims think of Jesus as a prophet like the Old Testament Abraham. In their system of belief, God's great prophet was Mohammed, born in the Middle Eastern city of Mecca in about A.D. 570.

Even within a single religion, dogmatic differences persist. Roman Catholics believe that during the holy sacrament of communion, bread and wine change mystically into the body and blood of Christ. Most Protestants think of the bread and wine as symbols only. Members of many Baptist and other conservative or fundamentalist churches regard every word in the Bible as literally true. God's creation of the earth in six days; Eve's temptation by the serpent in the Garden of Eden; the slaying of Abel by his brother, Cain; the deceit Rebekah and her son Jacob practiced upon Isaac — all happened exactly as it is written down, fundamentalists believe. But most nonfundamentalist Christians, and members of the Jewish faith as well, see the Bible as a collection of ancient myths, poetry and wisdom, lovely and inspiring, but not actual fact.

It is not hard to imagine such ideas and dogmas creeping into ethics lessons in public schools. Religious people hold their beliefs deeply, rarely making an effort to conceal them. And although religious instruction is supposed to play no part whatsoever in U.S. public school life, it often has. Until the U.S. Supreme Court banned the practice in 1962, nearly every teacher in the country led his or her class in prayer, Christian prayer, at the start of each school day. Even now, many school districts observe a daily moment of silence, during which students may pray or meditate. Attempts have also been made, generally by the leaders of fundamentalist Christian sects, to get schools to order the teaching of certain dogmatic ideas, such as the creation story as it is told in the Bible. As recently as 1987, a Louisiana law required the public school teaching of creationism along with the scientific theory of evolution. Given some sects' history of trying to force religious instruction into the classroom, it is no wonder many Americans fear that asking schools to teach ethics will mean letting them indoctrinate children with this or that particular religious belief at the same time.

Perhaps it will turn out that way, but it needn't, not if people are clear about what religion is and what ethics is and how they are different.

Although ethics is part of all religions, it is broader than any single religion. Ethics does not concern itself with whether or not Jesus was the Messiah or whether God created the earth in six days. These are matters of dogma. Ethics is more. Ethics stands at the point where narrow religious distinctions disappear and where that which unites all religions — humankind's desire to live according to universal standards of right and wrong — begins. Ethics does not say, as Islam does, that people must bow toward Mohammed's city of Mecca five times a day to pray. It says, Love thy neighbor. Ethics does not insist on belief in the miracle of communion or the literal truth of the Bible. But it does ask us to live by the Golden Rule.

The Golden Rule lies at the heart of what ethics has in common with religion. "All things whatsoever you would that men should do to you, do you even so to them," says Christianity. Buddhism says the same: "Hurt not others in what that you yourself would find hurtful."

Confucianism puts the thought in its own words: "Do not unto others what you would not have them do unto you." And so does Judaism: "What is hateful to you, do not to your fellow man." The exhortation is the same for the followers of Taoism: "Regard your neighbor's gain as your own gain, and your neighbor's loss as your own loss."

The lesson of the Golden Rule is one that schools ought to be teaching, grade schools as well as high schools and colleges, more and more Americans are coming to think. Among those who have expressed the thought most forcefully is William J. Bennett, secretary of education in the Reagan administration. Students need to become "morally literate," Bennett told a New York group in 1986.

Bennett, a Republican and a political conservative, was joined in his call for moral education by New York's liberal Democratic governor, Mario Cuomo. "When you get kids for eight years in an elementary school and you never say anything to them about values, I suspect what you're saying to them is 'there are no values,' '' Cuomo said. What values would the governor have the schools teach? Compassion, a sense of personal worth, respect for each individual's rights, awareness of the equality of all Americans, an understanding of the importance of working for a common good greater than one's personal interest, respect for the law and a love of country, he answered. Or, more succinctly, to put the welfare of others, and of society as a whole, ahead of self.

7
Truth — and Honesty

Cr-r-rack! The baseball flies off the end of the bat and up the infield. The runner on third breaks for the plate. Feet pounding, he races down the base path. The crowd roars; it's the bottom of the ninth inning in a tie game, and if the man scores, the home team will win the World Series.

Now, though, the other team's shortstop is moving. He stabs backhand at the ball, snares it, whirls and braces himself to make the throw. Straight into the catcher's mitt! The catcher makes a swipe at the runner, who hits the dirt and slides safely under the tag.

The crowd goes mad. The championship is theirs.

"Out!" yells the umpire.

Out? It cannot be. The runner beat the throw, touched home base. That is what happened and the crowd knows it. The runner does, too. Waving his arms, he stamps over to the angry knot of players gathered around the umpire. The other umps converge on the scene. Will they change the call? Furiously, each team argues for its point of view, its version of the truth. No one lies; each speaks for the truth as he sees it.

What is the truth? Around the country, fans who've been following the action on television watch the videotaped replay. There it all is again: the hit, the throw to home, the slide. And what about the tag? Did the catcher make the play or did he not? Over and over, the replay is repeated, first from this camera angle, then from that. With each showing, the truth becomes less certain. From the position of the camera stationed behind home plate, it looks as if the tag was successful. From the center field camera, the runner appeared to have touched base a split second before the catcher completed the play. Even the game's announcers are not sure of the call. What is the truth in this particular case?

It may never be known, not definitely. Nor is it only in baseball that the truth is sometimes unknowable. Doctors who fail to tell patients the full truth about their illnesses may do so because they themselves do not fully comprehend the truth. Think of the physicians who tried to treat the world's first AIDS patients back in the 1970s, before the disease had been recognized or given a name. All that those doctors would have known was that they were seeing some strange conditions: rare cancers combined with unusual infections or debilitating anemias, for example. What, they must have wondered, could account for such diverse symptoms? What "truth" could they have told their patients?

Or take a scientist who is trying to prepare a report on the environmental hazards of a chemical poison like dioxin. Dioxin is very, very toxic. That's a well-known truth, but what precise effect can the substance be expected to have on people exposed to tiny amounts of it? Is there any safe level of exposure? If so, what? Research may one day reveal the answers, but for now, the scientist knows, the truth is hidden.

Even when the truth is knowable, it may be difficult — or impossible — for people to recognize it. That is because their personal experiences or prejudices may obscure their perceptions. Think of a Jewish survivor of Adolf Hitler's Nazi Germany. That person may have spent time in a concentration camp, been released, moved to the United States and lived there for forty years. But isn't his understanding of events always going to be colored by his terrible experiences? Won't he, for example, tend to be supersensitive to hints of anti-Jewish feeling? Perhaps one of his Christian friends refuses to sponsor him for membership in an exclusive club, offering as an excuse the fact that he himself has belonged for only a short time. To the survivor, that excuse may appear to be a lie and an insult to his race and religion. To his American-born wife, it may seem no more than an unimportant social snub — or even the simple truth.

The fact that human beings often view the truth through a veil of preconceptions and prejudgments has important implications for public life as well. Among those who did the most to heighten Americans' awareness of the problem of missing children — and to raise exaggerated concerns about the number of yearly disappearances — was a Florida couple whose young son vanished while out shopping with his mother. Later, the boy was found murdered. It should not surprise anyone that his parents were especially sensitive to the problem.

The debate over the use of nuclear energy to generate electricity is another public policy area in which truth-obscuring prejudice makes itself felt. Many proponents of the technology are men and women who have worked with it for years and who feel comfortable doing so. For them, the truth is that nuclear energy is the best way America has to meet its energy demands. That version of the truth is reflected in their vocabulary. Nuclear plants are "safe" and "clean." Accidents are not accidents but "transients," "normal aberrations" or "abnormal evolutions."

To those Americans who oppose continued reliance on nuclear energy, on the other hand, the truth is that the technology is deadly dangerous. One of their particular concerns is the radioactive element plutonium, produced in the nuclear chain reaction that powers the electric generators. Antinuclear activists rarely mention the word "plutonium" without prefacing it by "hazardous," "deadly," "lethal" or "toxic."

The debate over what the truth really is goes beyond vocabulary. According to Dr. Helen Caldicott, a leading U.S. nuclear critic, "One pound [of plutonium], if uniformly distributed, could hypothetically induce lung cancer in every person on earth." But to a pronuclear trade group called the Atomic Industrial Forum (AIF), "Plutonium is not particularly *hazardous:* it cannot harm people it cannot touch."

Who has hold of the truth here? The AIF is perfectly correct; plutonium will not hurt anyone it doesn't touch. Neither will a forty-car freight train speeding along at fifty miles an hour. That does not mean the train is not dangerous, though, or that people should not do everything they can to stay out of its way. Caldicott is right, too. Statistically, a pound of plutonium could kill off the population of the globe. But who would want to be the one assigned to the impossible task of arranging its "uniform" distribution? Although both Caldicott and the AIF are telling the truth, neither is being entirely truthful. Or rather, neither is telling the whole truth.

Neither of them could. The whole truth, about the nuclear power industry or anything else, is beyond human understanding. Who can say what nuclear accidents lie ahead for the world, what future energy needs will be, what innovative technologies will emerge, what medical treatments on radiation poisoning will be discovered, what new hazards will crop up? No one. But people would have to know all that — and more — before they could claim to know the whole truth about the dangers and benefits nuclear power has to offer.

What do we mean by "the whole truth," anyway? What is truth?

Many have asked that question. Pontius Pilate, the Roman governor of Judaea, asked it of Jesus nearly two thousand years ago. "For this cause came I into the world," Jesus had said during his trial before Pilate, "that I should bear witness unto the truth." Pilate did not understand. "What is truth?" he wanted to know. But Jesus gave no answer.

What is truth? Like Pilate, we do not, cannot, know. We are only human, after all. But being human, we sometimes make the mistake of thinking that the truth is exactly what we do know. When that happens, trouble usually follows.

People on each side of the nuclear power debate believe they know the truth about that issue, and together, they confuse the public in a war of semi-truths and half-lies. In the 1950s, members of the Eisenhower administration thought they knew the truth about what was best for the nations and peoples of Southeast Asia. They acted — deceitfully — on that truth. A few years later, Lyndon Johnson and others told the country the truth, their truth, about what needed doing in Vietnam. We know what that truth led to. Anti-abortionists "know" the truth and some use it in an effort to deprive American women of a right that is legally theirs. Doctors, lawyers, scientists — and all the rest of us, too — sometimes do tremendous harm through what they, and we, "know" to be true.

If absolute truth is unknowable, does that mean we must get along without truth? Of course not. Life must be built on truth or become unlivable. And people can build on truth — by being honest.

Being honest means coming as close to the truth as we can, as often as we can. But it also means accepting the fact that that truth is not absolute. It means being willing to listen to the truth as others see and tell it. It means considering their versions of the truth along with our own. Being honest means being direct and forthcoming, open-minded and tolerant, treating others as we hope they will treat us. It means thinking, speaking and acting ethically.

Truth, complete and utter truth, is beyond the human ability to grasp, but honesty is well within our reach. And it is still the best policy.

Index